PRACTICAL
SOCIAL WORK

THE UNIVERS'
WINCHF

Series Editor: Jo Campling

BASW

Editorial Advisory Board:
Robert Adams, Terry Bamford, Charles Barker,
Lena Dominelli, Malcolm Payne, Michael Preston-Shoot,
Daphne Statham and Jane Tunstill

Social work is at an important stage in its development. All professions must be responsive to changing social and economic conditions if they are to meet the needs of those they serve. This series focuses on sound practice and the specific contribution which social workers can make to the well-being of our society.

The British Association of Social Workers has always been conscious of its role in setting guidelines for practice and in seeking to raise professional standards. The conception of the Practical Social Work series arose from a survey of BASW members to discover where they, the practitioners in social work, felt there was the most need for new literature. The response was overwhelming and enthusiastic, and the result is carefully planned, coherent series of books. The emphasis is firmly on practice set in a theoretical framework. The books will inform, stimulate and promote discussion, thus adding to the further development of skills and high professional standards. All the authors are practitioners and teachers of social work representing a wide variety of experience.

JO CAMPLING

A list of published titles in this series follows overleaf

PRACTICAL SOCIAL WORK

Robert Adams *Self-Help, Social Work and Empowerment*

David Anderson *Social Work and Mental Handicap*

James G. Barber *Beyond Casework*

James G. Barber *Social Work with Addictions*

Peter Beresford and Suzy Croft *Citizen Involvement: A Practical Guide for Change*

Suzy Braye and Michael Preston-Shoot *Practising Social Work Law*

Robert Brown, Stanley Bute and Peter Ford *Social Workers at Risk*

Alan Butler and Colin Pritchard *Social Work and Mental Illness*

Crescy Cannan, Lynne Berry and Karen Lyons *Social Work and Europe*

Roger Clough *Residential Work*

David M. Cooper and David Ball *Social Work and Child Abuse*

Veronica Coulshed *Management in Social Work*

Veronica Coulshed *Social Work Practice: An Introduction (2nd edn)*

Paul Daniel and John Wheeler *Social Work and Local Politics*

Peter R. Day *Sociology in Social Work Practice*

Lena Dominelli *Anti-Racist Social Work: A Challenge for White Practitioners and Educators*

Celia Doyle *Working with Abused Children*

Angela Everitt, Pauline Hardiker, Jane Littlewood and Audrey Mullender *Applied Research for Better Practice*

Kathy Ford and Alan Jones *Student Supervision*

David Francis and Paul Henderson *Working with Rural Communities*

Michael D. A. Freeman *Children, their Families and the Law*

Alison Froggatt *Family Work with Elderly People*

Danya Glaser and Stephen Frosh *Child Sexual Abuse (2nd edn)*

Bryan Glastonbury *Computers in Social Work*

Gill Gorell Barnes *Working with Families*

Cordelia Grimwood and Ruth Popplestone *Women, Management and Care*

Jalna Hanmer and Daphne Statham *Women and Social Work: Towards a Woman-Centred Practice*

Tony Jeffs and Mark Smith (eds) *Youth Work*

Michael Kerfoot and Alan Butler *Problems of Childhood and Adolescence*

Joyce Lishman *Communication in Social Work*

Carol Lupton and Terry Gillespie (eds) *Working with Violence*

Mary Marshall *Social Work with Old People (2nd edn)*

Paula Nicolson and Rowan Bayne *Applied Psychology for Social Workers (2nd edn)*

Kieran O'Hagan *Crisis Intervention in Social Services*

Michael Oliver *Social Work with Disabled People*

Joan Orme and Bryan Glastonbury *Care Management: Tasks and Workloads*

Malcolm Payne *Social Care in the Community*

Malcolm Payne *Working in Teams*

John Pitts *Working with Young Offenders*

Michael Preston-Shoot *Effective Groupwork*

Peter Raynor, David Smith and Maurice Vanstone *Effective Probation Practice*

Carole R. Smith *Adoption and Fostering: Why and How*

Carole R. Smith *Social Work with the Dying and Bereaved*

Carole R. Smith, Marty T. Lane and Terry Walsh *Child Care and the Courts*

David Smith *Criminology for Social Work*

Gill Stewart and John Stewart *Social Work and Housing*

Christine Stones *Focus on Families*

Neil Thompson *Anti-Discriminatory Practice*

Neil Thompson, Michael Murphy and Steve Stradling *Dealing with Stress*

Derek Tilbury *Working with Mental Illness*

Alan Twelvetrees *Community Work (2nd edn)*

Hilary Walker and Bill Beaumount (eds) *Working with Offenders*

Effective Probation Practice

Peter Raynor
David Smith
and
Maurice Vanstone

MACMILLAN

First published 1994 by
MACMILLAN PRESS LTD
Houndmills, Basingstoke, Hampshire RG21 2XS
and London
Companies and representatives
throughout the world

ISBN 0–333–58523–2 hardcover
ISBN 0–333–58524–0 paperback

A catalogue record for this book is available
from the British Library.

10   9   8   7   6   5   4   3   2
03   02   01   00   99   98   97   96   95

Printed in Malaysia

Series Standing Order (Practical Social Work)

If you would like to receive future titles in this series as they are published, you can make
use of our standing order facility. To place a standing order please contact your
bookseller or, in case of difficulty,write to us at the address below with your name and
address and the name of the series. Please state with which title you wish to begin your
standing order. (If you live outside the United Kingdom we may not have the rights for
your area, in which case we will forward your order to the publisher concerned.)

Standing Order Service, Macmillan Distribution Ltd
Houndmills, Basingstoke, Hampshire RG21 2XS, England

To the memory of William Martin Vanstone

Contents

viii   *Contents*

Acknowledgements

Many people have helped us to write this book. Individually and collectively, we want to thank the Chief Officer, staff and clients of the Mid-Glamorgan Probation Service for their collaboration in and contribution to the STOP study, and Jacqueline Lucas, who worked as a research assistant on the survey of staff views; the Director and staff of the Institute of Criminology in Cambridge for their help and hospitality during Peter Raynor's Visiting Fellowship, which allowed him to take part in the research on the quality of social inquiry and pre-sentence reports; Loraine Gelsthorpe and Andrea Tisi, the co-researchers on these studies; the Home Office Research and Planning Unit for financial support of the work on social inquiry and pre-sentence reports, and of the staff survey element of the STOP evaluation; National Children's Home for supporting the work on social inquiry reports in Scotland; and Bruce Seymour, Rob Thomas, Sue Thomas, Courtney Warner and other colleagues and students, past and present, whose contribution to the development of our ideas has been incalculable. We owe special debts to Anna Javed and Jacky Smith, of the Lancashire and South Yorkshire Probation Services, for reading parts of the book and for their stimulating comments; to Jen Fletcher for turning our varied typescripts into something presentable; and to our spouses and children, for putting up with us, and more than that. The failings of the book are of course solely our responsibility.

PETER RAYNOR
DAVID SMITH
MAURICE VANSTONE

Introduction

In this book we aim to put forward a positive and realistic view, informed by an analysis of current government policy, of the future contribution of the probation service to the criminal justice system. We discuss the purposes of this service in terms of influencing sentencers, providing help to people on probation that is offence-focused, but does not neglect other problems, and contributing to a broader community response to crime and its associated problems. We outline the kind of management structure which will help probation officers to work effectively in each of these areas. The book is informed throughout by recent research on 'what works' – not only in reducing the risk of reconviction, but in intervening in court, and in developing strategies for crime prevention and community cohesion. We hope that our commitment to anti-discriminatory practice is an equally pervasive influence; rather than segregating this into chapters labelled 'race' and 'gender', we have tried to embed it in our discussion of the various themes which contribute to our argument.

In saying this we acknowledge that there are other forms of discrimination – ageism, disablism, homophobia – on which we have little to say. This does not mean that we consider them unimportant, but at present there is no substantial research on how they operate within the criminal justice system which would allow us to discuss them helpfully, or even to direct the reader elsewhere. In so far as we can make statements about discrimination in criminal justice on the basis of age, it seems that it is more likely that it works benignly than otherwise, if one assumes that being diverted from prosecution is preferable to prosecution, from the recipient's point of view. In relation to issues of disability, we are aware that many people with whom the probation service works suffer from disabilities (Stewart *et al*,

1

1989) which make them vulnerable to discrimination, especially because they may be seen as self-inflicted, for example through substance abuse or road traffic accidents; and probation officers have a responsibility not to compound these people's problems by practising, or colluding with, discrimination. On homophobia and heterosexism, we are clear that if we had been discussing work in prisons these forms of discrimination would have been highly relevant, and we are also aware that the culture of machismo and stereotypical masculinity requires consideration in any attempt to explain crime and criminality. These matters are, however, largely beyond the scope of this book. Rather than continually listing forms of discrimination in a tokenistic way, we have concentrated on racism and sexism; there is a well-established research literature on the ways in which black people and women experience discrimination in criminal justice, and on how this might be tackled in practice.

Our approach has been to explore each of our core themes in depth, rather than to attempt a survey of the whole range of probation officers' work. Thus there is nothing in this book about the specialism of civil work (which would require a substantial text to itself), and nothing that bears directly on throughcare or aftercare, or community service, though we believe that our proposed offender-centred strategy, and the methods we suggest for effective practice with people on probation, may also be relevant to work with people in prison or recently released from it. The distinctive practice issues of work with prisoners have recently been discussed by Williams (1992), and the after-care literature has been reviewed by Haines (1990); both will be useful to readers specifically interested in these topics.

The book is structured as follows. Chapter 1 discusses recent (and continuing) government efforts to reduce the prison population, and explores the implications for probation practice of 'just deserts' sentencing as embodied in the 1991 Criminal Justice Act. Chapter 2 sets the current position of the service in context by tracing how we got where we are today. The changing policy and organisational contexts of practice are explored, and it is argued that instead of the diversity and piecemeal innovation that have been typical of the service's response hitherto, we need an approach which is more empirically informed, and clearer about values, purpose and methods.

Chapter 3 focuses on court reports as the main means by which probation officers can hope to influence sentencing. The features of good (and bad) reporting practice are discussed in the context of recent experience, especially in juvenile justice, and in the light of the new demands of the 1991 Act. These themes are developed in Chapter 4, which draws on recent research to suggest rational ways of judging the quality of pre-sentence reports. A strategy for gate-keeping and monitoring is outlined which should help promote consistent, anti-discriminatory and effective practice.

Chapter 5 turns to issues of supervision and help for offenders. It argues that much recent work shows that the pessimistic message that 'nothing works' is no longer true (if it ever was). It is, rather, possible to specify quite closely what the character-istics of effective work with offenders are. 'Effectiveness' here means not only the reduction of offending but help with other problems, and a practical commitment to anti-discriminatory practice. Chapter 6 draws on new research, in which two of the authors have been closely involved, concerning the effectiveness of a particular model of work, the 'reasoning and rehabilitation' approach (Ross *et al.*, 1988). It explores practical issues of im-plementing and evaluating a new programme, in terms both of its effectiveness in helping to bring about change in individuals and of its impact on the criminal justice system.

Chapter 7 broadens the focus to explore the possible contri-bution of the probation service to alleviating problems associated with crime in the wider community. Various attempts to make practical sense of the idea of 'community involvement' are ex-plored, and set within their changing policy contexts. The discus-sion recognises the difficulties the service faces in working with communities which are often deprived and divided, but identifies successful and promising initiatives in the fields of crime prevention and victim-offender mediation.

Chapter 8 discusses what kind of management and organisa-tional structure the service needs if it is to realise the prospect presented in earlier chapters – of consistent, effective, well informed and anti-discriminatory practice. It is argued that the managerialism which has been the service's main response to growing size and complexity can stifle rather than promote creativity and innovation. Drawing on recent examples and on experience in training and staff development, the chapter outlines a model of open management and leadership designed to maintain the service's value base while enabling it to respond creatively to demands for change.

1

Probation in Penal Policy: Welfare, Justice or Crime Reduction?

Introduction

The metaphor of 'moving the probation service to centre stage' has been deployed many times by government spokespersons in the last four years, usually in a way which combines the promise of a starring role with more than a hint of menace about what might happen if the offer is not accepted. The threats have included marginalisation, privatisation, the hiving-off of core tasks reorganisation into a national service directively managed from the Home Office, and the re-structuring of probation training to reduce a presumed excessive exposure to the culture and values of social work. An unprecedented scrutiny and critique of probation management and practice has been embodied in six government policy papers (Home Office, 1988, 1990a, 1990b, 1990c, 1991a and 1992a), two Audit reports (Audit Commission, 1989; National Audit Office, 1989) and innumerable speeches and statements; many of these seemed to be designed to reassure the government's political supporters that an interest in the probation service did not mean going soft on crime or on value for money. Small wonder if their impact within the service was far from reassuring: the problem with a centre-stage role is that it

5

attracts the spotlight, and suspicion of the government's motives or hostility to its wider policies were, for some, reinforced by a nostalgia for more comfortable times when governments showed less interest in what probation officers did.

A major reason for producing this book is the authors' shared belief that the opportunities created by new penal policies and the 'centre-stage role' are real and positive. The new policies originate from a Conservative Government not noted for the generosity of its social legislation, and this is reflected in a limited understanding of the social context of crime and of the impact of poverty and unemployment on potential offenders. Nevertheless, this book aims to set out some of the sober and realistic reasons for believing that the challenge of new legislation can be met, and to identify some of the strategies and methods which seem to hold out the best hopes of effectiveness in current circumstances, and the current state of our knowledge.

Fears, doubts and grounds for hope

The experience of the 1980s has been particularly rich in sources of doubt and uncertainty and, paradoxically, in grounds for guarded optimism. In the late 1970s and early 1980s several writers (particularly Bottoms and McWilliams, 1979; and Raynor, 1985) tried to respond to the climate of scepticism generated by negative research findings about the effectiveness of the usual forms of supervision in reducing reconviction rates; they rejected the claims of probation to provide a quasi-medical or quasi-psychiatric 'treatment' for offenders who were presumed incapable of self-direction (see, for example, Foren and Bailey, 1968), and advocated instead a more open and explicit form of practice based on a dual approach to the social work role: on the one hand, helping offenders to address and resolve problems (for themselves and others) associated with their offending, and on the other hand influencing the criminal justice system itself to seek and use more constructive or less harmful responses to

crime in the interests of offenders, victims and the communities in which they live. Other writers (for example, Walker and Beaumont, 1981, 1985) adopted a specifically Marxist or socialist critique of the criminal justice system, and while they are open to the charge of 'left idealism' in their tendency to see crime as a threat to the State and social order rather than as a further element in the deprivation and victimisation of the poorest and most vulnerable, they helped to create a climate of opinion in which practitioners became more aware of specific oppressive features of criminal justice processes: for example, in their impact on black people or on women. The practical strategies advocated by the political radicals (for example, Hugman, 1980) actually differed little from those which made sense within the 'non-treatment' approach, but what both had in common was their reliance on ethical or ideological arguments in the absence, to begin with, of really convincing empirical demonstrations that practice based on these models would prove more effective. Some advocates of 'non-treatment' argued explicitly in favour of trying to avoid negative impacts (doing less harm) rather than seeking positive changes (doing more good), while others made the most of a small number of documented hopeful projects as pointers to effective strategies.

The Home Office, meanwhile, presented itself as unconvinced: at one stage the senior civil servant most closely identified with new strategies in criminal justice told an audience of chief probation officers that not only was there no evidence that an increase in probation expenditure would bring any 'added value in terms of results', there was no evidence either that a reduction would do any harm (Faulkner, 1986). Officials and Ministers also faced the more pressing problem of a prison population which continued to rise despite new non-custodial sentences (such as Community Service) and ineffective deterrent gestures (such as the ill-starred 'short sharp shock' experiment in the Detention Centres: see Thornton *et al.*, 1984). The need to control public expenditure, as well as a reasonable preference for doing less harm, combined to suggest a more positive view of the probation service's potential

contribution, and in 1984 the Home Office issued the first 'Statement of National Objectives and Priorities' for the probation service. This clearly implied that the future role of the probation service lay in developing and providing forms of supervision in the community for offenders who would otherwise receive custodial sentences, and led directly to the development of 'performance indicators' for probation services. These required services to monitor and report, for example, the proportion of probationers who had previous convictions and previous custodial experience; higher proportions of these would indicate that the service was supervising offenders in the community whose records would otherwise have incurred a substantial risk of a custodial sentence. A variety of such indicators were used in an attempt to assess how far the aim of limiting custody was being achieved and, as described in the next chapter, they both provoked some resistance and helped to create a working culture in which information mattered.

The re-emergence of effectiveness

The belief that results of this kind might be achievable was largely a consequence of what must be regarded, with hindsight, as one of the most remarkable practitioner-led changes in British social policy. This was the discovery that social work practice in the field of juvenile offenders could, through a conscious and organised strategy of influencing decision-making in local criminal justice systems, achieve a dramatic reduction in the use of expensive and damaging custodial sentences and residential care (Blagg and Smith, 1989; Morris and Giller, 1987). This strategy owed something to criminological insights about avoidance of labelling and stigma (Thorpe *et al.*, 1980) as well as to a pragmatic recognition that most young people would grow out of offending (Rutherford, 1986) if the excesses of well-meaning compulsory social work could be avoided. The implications of such 'system strategies' for probation practice are explored in Chapter 3; their impact on Government policy

towards the probation service was to encourage a similar approach to young adult offenders, and in 1986 the rate of custodial sentencing of young adults began to fall, just as the number of juveniles in custody had begun to fall five years before.

These strategies had developed outside the probation service and were based more on 'harm avoidance' than on the expectation of lower reconvictions; even 'alternative to custody' programmes of supervision for juvenile offenders were often evaluated more in relation to their impact on local juvenile justice systems (for example, by assessing how many custodial sentences had been avoided) than in relation to their effects on offending. Many probation officers were sceptical about strategies which seemed research-based and 'academic', and to rely more on adherence to an agreed strategy than on the individualistic version of practitioner autonomy which was still the norm in the probation service; others saw important differences between working with juveniles who were confidently expected, in most cases, to 'grow out of crime', and working with the adult clients of the probation service who often seemed to have missed their chance to do so. The influence of the new ideas on probation practice was slow and patchy, often depending, like so much else, on the enthusiasm and interest of particular officers. Nevertheless, the impact on probation was to be profound, largely because the success of juvenile justice policy and practice transformed the official view of what social workers in the criminal justice system could achieve.

The other major development which contributed, during the late 1980s and the beginning of the 1990s, to a more optimistic view of the probation service's possible effectiveness was the emergence of positive findings from some evaluative studies of current probation projects. Although few in number, these studies have tended to concentrate on responses to problems which have quite a high policy profile, such as intensive supervision programmes for young adult offenders in England and Wales (Raynor, 1988; Roberts, 1989) and Community Service in Scotland (McIvor, 1992). These studies have shown evidence of an impact on levels of reoffending, at least in comparison with the reoffending which would have been expected following other disposals, and have coincided with a greater international interest not only in reviewing relevant research (for example, Gendreau and Ross, 1979; McIvor, 1990; Andrews *et al.*, 1990) but in carrying out new studies (for example, Ross *et al.*, 1988) in which positive outcomes are no longer a rarity. Improvements in methodology have led to greater confidence in the available positive findings, and even some classics of the 'nothing works' movement have been reappraised. As Robert Martinson himself put it a few years after publishing his major sceptical review (Lipton *et al.*, 1975), the original conclusions had been exaggerated:

> On the basis of the evidence in our current study, I withdraw this conclusion. I have often said that treatment added to ... criminal justice is 'impotent' and I withdraw this characterization as well. I protested at the slogan used by the media to sum up what I said – 'nothing works' ... the conclusion is not correct.   (Martinson, 1979)

The doctrine that 'nothing works' is now untenable and demonstrably false; this does not, however, mean that everything works. Such an assumption would be, if anything, more dangerous than its opposite, and would risk a return to a version of the discredited 'treatment model' which justified coercive intervention by reference to eventual benefits of a largely theoretical or imaginary kind. The evidence is that some things can work, particularly if well done, but they are not necessarily the kind of thing which the probation service has traditionally done, nor are they necessarily cheap or easily replicable. Chapters 5 and 6 explore some practical implications of recent and current research; for the present, it is sufficient to note that under some circumstances the doctrine that 'everything works' might be just as convenient to a cost-cutting administration as its opposite, since both reduce the need to distinguish between effective and ineffective programmes and to make the consequent selective investment in quality.

Methods, policies and values

One further risk of preoccupation with technical effectiveness, with 'what works', is that the necessary debate about means can displace and substitute for the equally necessary debate about ends: effectiveness in achieving what? Our assumptions about purposes shape the goals of our organisations and of individual practitioners, and also shape our choice of evaluative criteria and performance indicators. Even crime reduction through avoidance of reconviction is not necessarily the ultimate test, since there might be ways to achieve this which are ethically unacceptable, and there will certainly be a choice of strategies with different implications for individual freedom and quality of life: for example, choices between empowering people through acquisition of new skills to make a crime-free lifestyle more feasible, and incapacitating them through a reduction of opportunities both for offending and for a normal and satisfying life. Most probation projects (but not all: see Kent Probation Service, 1981) have at least aspired to the former option; developments such as electronically monitored curfew orders point more towards the latter approach, and debates about their acceptability are not simply technical debates about effectiveness.

Government messages about the values and goals of probation tended to shift in the early 1990s, possibly as a result of an increasingly positive view of the service's potential usefulness. The policy statements which punctuated the late 1980s and early 1990s underwent a subtle change of emphasis from the first Green Paper (Home Office, 1988), which sought to display a vision of 'punishment in the community' and to castigate probation services for a soft approach which treated offenders as victims of society in need of help. This earned the almost unanimous hostility of practitioners despite a clear statement of opposition to the continuing over-use of custody (for example, 'imprisonment is not the most effective punishment for most crime'). By the time policy had moved on to the White Paper stage the purposes of supervision had come to include the 'reintegration of the offender with the community' (Home

Office, 1990a) and the resulting legislation actually identifies 'securing the rehabilitation of the offender' as part of the statutory purpose of probation supervision (1991 Criminal Justice Act, section 8). The subsequent draft 'Statement of Purpose' went even further, identifying a core aim of the probation service as the reduction of crime through the rehabilitation of offenders (Home Office, 1992b). Such a recognition would have seemed a major victory for probation at the time of the first Green Paper, and represents a degree of success in persuading the government to re-examine some of its earlier positions; to some extent these may be changes of presentation, but this is not unimportant if, as Rumgay (1989) argues, the language helps to shape attitudes and practice. The debate about the purposes and values of probation is as lively and relevant as ever, now that it has become more empirically informed. This debate must now be set in a new context, as practitioners throughout a diverse and fragmented criminal justice 'system' try to make sense of their own versions of justice in the light of a new Criminal Justice Act.

Welfare, justice and the Criminal Justice Act

Traditionally social work services in the criminal justice system have had to negotiate the conflict between 'welfare' models based on the 'needs' of offenders or 'clients' (often, in practice, needs attributed by professionals rather than identified by themselves) and 'justice' models which stress fairness and consistency of response proportionate to the 'badness' of the offence. The relative strengths and weaknesses of these models as guides to practice have been thoroughly explored in the social work literature of the 1980s (for example, Thorpe *et al.*, 1980; Raynor, 1985; Harris and Webb, 1987; Rutherford, 1986). To summarise and no doubt over-simplify a complex argument, welfare models risk well-meaning but harmful over-intervention on the basis of presumed needs ('it's for your own good'). Justice models tend to limit intervention to no more than the seriousness of the offence deserves, but offer little guidance about offenders' needs or about how to deal fairly with people committing similar offences in the context of very different backgrounds and circumstances, where common sense would attribute different amounts of blame. The new Act, by explicitly adopting for the first time in Britain a version of the justice model and starting from the principle that sentencing should be proportionate to current offending, is seeking to avoid one particular kind of injustice: it seeks to ensure that persistent minor offenders will no longer incur disproportionately severe punishment on the basis of their past record of offences for which they have already been punished. Instead of the usual pragmatism and muddle, we now have criminal justice legislation actually based on a theoretical view, however limited and incomplete, and a moral position about the proper nature of criminal justice. Current and future debates about the values and purposes of probation need now to be related to the models of criminal justice embodied in the new law.

In this context, it is important to recognise that the new Act embodies a modified version of 'just deserts' theory rather than a purist form. In extreme 'flat time' versions of the justice model, which relate given levels of penalty (usually imprisonment) inflexibly to particular offences, there is no room for individual differences, mitigation or consideration of the different circumstances or motives of people committing the same offence. A simplistic mechanical approach to 'justice' can invite extremely adverse social consequences through its failure to make these distinctions (for a detailed review of these arguments see Hudson, 1987). The 1991 Act, by contrast, departs from strict proportionality in a number of ways. For example, it allows longer sentences for dangerous offenders, and conversely it allows consideration of mitigating factors even where unrelated to the actual offence.

However, the Act remains vulnerable to some of the established criticisms of just deserts models: like the Green and White papers from which it developed, it tends to adopt a socially blind model of crime, seeing offending as a moral failing of individuals rather than as arising out of choices made (or

actions 'drifted into' – see Matza, 1964) in particular situations
and particular social contexts. Its concept of punishment is
similarly simplistic: punishment is seen as the standard response,
and this has led to much criticism from probation officers and
others concerned to develop constructive responses. It is important, however, to recognise what is implied by the Act's
model of punishment: punishment is identified as deprivation
or modification of liberty, rather than as the infliction of pain
or suffering which, as Nils Christie has reminded us (Christie,
1982), has traditionally been the underlying nature of
punishment.

The new Act, then, draws on a discourse of just deserts and
punishment, but in a way which leaves much more scope for
traditional probation concerns than its critics may originally
have feared. The idea of offenders as morally responsible is
nothing new to advocates of the non-treatment model, who
always emphasised a respect for individuals as decision-makers
and moral agents (Bottoms and McWilliams, 1979; Raynor,
1985). Similarly the idea of probation as containing an element
of punishment by virtue of the demands it makes on offenders,
rather than by virtue of painful or punitive content, would be
familiar to those who argued many years ago that a probation
order contained a dual contract: one between the probationer
and the court relating to compliance with supervision
requirements, and one (additional and voluntary) between
probationer and probation officer relating to help and assistance
if required (see, for instance, Bryant *et al.*, 1978). It also seems
likely that many probationers have always recognised an
element of penalty in the probation order. Those probation
officers who rightly pointed out in response to the 1988 Green
Paper that they had not been trained to administer punishment
may, in the end, have missed the point: nothing in the Act or the
associated White Paper requires them to deliver punitive content
in supervision, and even tough talk about challenge, demand
and 'confronting offending behaviour' was as much a reflection
of current developments in offence-focused probation work as a
message about Government expectations. The tough talk was in

any case noticeably less prevalent in the Act itself, in the 'National Standards' issued by the Home Office to guide probation practice (Home Office, 1992c) and in the approved training materials (Home Office, 1992d), largely, it seems, because of fairly successful use by probation service organisations of the opportunities offered in an extensive consultation process.

The clearest indication that the Act is framed to let probation service concerns in rather than to keep them out lies in the central role given to the pre-sentence report. Undeterred by any theoretical discomforts about the place of individualised social information in a 'just deserts' model, the Act creates here an opportunity to situate individual episodes of offending in a social and individual context informed by an understanding of circumstances, needs, attitudes, beliefs and resources. The opportunities presented here for probation practice are discussed in Chapters 3 and 4. In effect the Act offers, as some critics have pointed out, a simple vision of crime and justice which is uninformed by an understanding of social context or of reasons for offending other than individual wickedness; in this respect it reflects its political origins in a Government whose previous leader declared 'there is no such thing as society', and which has concentrated on market-led individual liberty rather than social solidarity and the meeting of welfare needs. On the other hand, the Act is drafted in such a way as to let social considerations back in through the space it leaves for the probation service to influence both individual decisions and system developments. A wider social role for the service is also sanctioned by the clear official expectation, set out in the 1984 Statement of National Objectives and Priorities and regularly reinforced since, that the probation service should be actively involved with other organisations at a community level helping to prevent crime and to influence the community's response to crime. Crime cannot be understood or dealt with in isolation from the rest of people's social experience, and Chapter 7 explores the rationale and potential of this wider community role.

Values in practice

If the Act creates more space for probation influence and concerns than some of its critics feared, it has little to say about how that influence should be exercised, and the probation service will need its own set of values, policies and strategies to inform its practice. This is not the place to engage in an extended debate about probation values and practice theories; one of the authors has attempted this before (Raynor, 1985) and much of that work seems still relevant in the context of the new legislation. However, the provision of social work services in the criminal justice system requires some base in values: what kind of criminal justice system is desirable? What kind of social values should it reflect and embody? As MacIntyre (1988) reminds us, models of justice and the institutions which embody and demonstrate them are not simply constituted by the societies and cultures that surround and underpin them: they are also 'constitutive of' their societies, helping to construct and reinforce the normative assumptions underlying everyday life. Nils Christie (1977) has made a similar point that involvement in dispute resolution by the parties most affected has the function of reinforcing social norms as well as offering opportunities of satisfaction for the people concerned. What kind of social norms should probation embody and reinforce? Some traditional answers to this include respect for persons, the promotion of alternatives to the coercive infliction of pain as a response to criminal justice conflicts, and the development of opportunities for offenders and others involved in the problem of crime to participate in constructive action in response to it.

Such value-based policies and practices are important not simply in themselves, but in the statements they make and exemplify about social norms. Recent writing in 'republican' criminology has tried to relate issues of criminal justice policy and practice to wider social policy in the way that our Criminal Justice Act fails to do (Braithwaite, 1989; Braithwaite and Pettit, 1990). These writings argue, for instance, that criminal justice policy based on the individualistic assumptions of classical liberalism which underpin modern Conservative thought neglects the need for a holistic approach which promotes integration and the active maintenance of those conditions necessary for full citizenship.

Increasingly this kind of perspective, based on notions of citizenship and participation, seems to be generating the kind of critical arguments and proposals which used to flow from the socialist aspirations of collectivism and solidarity, which seem for the time being to have limited electoral appeal. Social integration requires, for example, avoidance of the kind of social and economic policies which create an excluded 'underclass', the dangers of which have been noted by many commentators as experienced as Dahrendorf (1985) and Galbraith (1992). A society which segregates, excludes and stigmatises its less wealthy citizens, its welfare recipients and its potential offenders offers them little opportunity or motivation to behave in ways which preserve for others the benefits of a full participating citizenship from which they themselves are cut off. The implications of a social ethic of inclusion rather than exclusion have been explored for British social policy by writers like Bill Jordan (1989, 1990), and have not been without their influence on probation practice through the emphasis they place on open and explicit dialogue and negotiation about needs, rights, 'welfare shares' and the role of welfare professionals. A similar distinction is made in Chapter 7, where we point to differences between marginalising and integrative approaches to crime prevention. Some of the implications for criminal justice practice are discussed by the 'republican' criminologists under the heading of 'reintegration', or the establishment of a dialogic communication with offenders which offers them the opportunity for restoration to full moral status as participating citizens. This concept has been discussed in the context of 'reintegrative shaming' (Braithwaite, 1989) which conjures up unfortunate visions of public humiliation; this is, however, a misunderstanding of the argument, since such methods are means of exclusion rather than reintegration, and 'reintegrative shaming' is intended to refer to experiences which offer offenders the opportunity to reappraise past behaviour and reintegrate themselves. This is close to the traditional meaning of 'rehabilitation', which, as McWilliams and Pease (1990) reminds us, is concerned with regaining moral status as a member of a community rather than simply with reduction of offending (the problematic nature of 'community' and its implications for probation practice are discussed in Chapter 7).

Reducing coercion and promoting participation and conflict resolution in criminal justice are reintegrative strategies; they are also rehabilitative, and prefigure a less divided and less individualistic society. They reflect the assumption that conflicts are not necessarily zero-sum, but may be capable of management and resolution in ways that represent satisfactory outcomes for both parties. The same can be true of conflicts of ideas: not all apparent contradictions are insoluble. For example, one possible approach to integrating welfare and justice considerations is to argue that the 'size' of the sentencing 'package' (and consequently the degree of reduction of liberty involved) should be determined and limited by considerations of justice and proportionality, but that the content of the package (whether supervision, reparation, compensation or whatever) should be as constructive as possible, based where feasible on dialogue with the offender, and rehabilitative in aim and effect. Similarly there is no necessary conflict between welfare and crime reduction. On the contrary, where evaluative research has been carried out in such a way as to consider these questions, suggestive evidence has sometimes emerged that when supervision successfully addresses problems of concern to offenders, reductions in offending are more likely to result (Raynor, 1988; McIvor, 1991). However, it is by no means straightforward to address this range of desirable aims successfully. A principled probation practice will seek to develop the theories and methods to do so, and this book makes a number of suggestions in this direction. In particular, it reflects the authors' dual concern with helping individual offenders and improving the quality and effectiveness of criminal justice. It also reflects a shared conviction that the development of effective social work within the criminal justice system is not only feasible but desirable and necessary in the interests of offenders, victims and society as a whole.

2

An Offender-Centred Strategy

Before developing further the argument for a practice model based on a dual approach of influencing systems and helping people who offend, we need to examine the changes in the organisation and work of the probation service during the past thirty years. In doing so we will necessarily pay attention to the context of these changes and in particular the negative effect of the research findings of the 1970s and the evaluative vacuum within which, by and large, probation activity existed. We will concern ourselves with relevant aspects of the history of the service, but readers who want a broader historical account should refer to the authoritative and established work of others (Bochel, 1976; Haxby, 1978; McWilliams, 1983, 1985, 1987; Raynor, 1985). A necessary detail of our focus will be on the characteristics of the people with whom probation workers currently engage and the types of practice undertaken with those people. We will conclude the chapter by highlighting the key problems which need to be addressed if a dual approach is to be effective.

What change?

Perhaps by way of an apologia, before sifting yet again through the familiar subject of the probation service and change, we should reflect on what has not changed. Like their police court missionary forbears, late-twentieth-century probation workers still peddle their wares among the poor and disadvantaged sections of the community; a majority retain a desire to do good; their core activities are still located within a spectrum of interest in crime and its psychological and sociological contexts. Despite the fears and doubts described in Chapter 1, the ideal of service is surviving with a resilience and strength which suggests that the notion of a 'probation force' lingers only as a chimera in the mind's eye of some future hardline Home Secretary. That service remains delivered to the courts, people who offend and, albeit indirectly, to the community. Whilst delivering it probation workers continue to struggle with the problem of gaining people's trust and winning their co-operation within a framework of judicially prescribed constraints.

The changes that have occurred have been, like changes in people, stimulated by the occasional dramatic event but mainly by less perceptible and more gradual shifts in emphasis and direction. We have described how in the past twenty five years the service has been influenced by the optimism of the sixties, the pessimism of the seventies, the 'right realism' of the eighties and the 'left realism' of the late eighties and early nineties, and move on now to examine what has changed at the level of practice.

What people?

In order to understand the nature of these changes we have to cast our eyes across the landscape of penal policy in the past thirty years or so. What kinds of probation worker and probation clients inhabited that landscape between the optimism of the Streatfeild report (Home Office, 1961) and the pessimism of the IMPACT experiment of 1974 (Folkard *et al.*, 1976)? As they are today, probation officers were almost exclusively white. Their supervisors were almost exclusively male, and many officers were untrained people who came directly into the service from a range of occupations. Their motivations clustered around the concept of help, and they were likely to talk more often than their modern counterparts about a sense of vocation. Whether through training or through the influence of the organisational culture, they were believers (to varying degrees) in the concept of casework, with its psychotherapeutic focus on unconscious processes and feelings. They were relieved, apparently, of the need to pay attention to material problems by the affluence of the post-war years, at least according to King (1958)!

In order to form a picture of the average probation client of those years it is necessary to find a path through the labyrinth of psychotherapeutic jargon. Beyond the talk of transference and deep-rooted and unconscious feelings, a picture does emerge of people who, because of familiar problems ranging from health to unemployment to debt, needed help. However, there was a strong possibility that they would be first or second offenders placed on probation primarily because of welfare considerations. The people who were to demand growing attention from the probation service of the eighties were as yet distanced from probation officers by their status as recidivists:

There is a further group of offenders who, whilst they do not often become subject of probation orders, are to be met in the higher courts; these are the 'professional criminals' who appear to have consciously chosen a life of crime and so become persistent offenders. (King, 1958, p. 85)

The only interventionist community-based sentence was the standard probation order, and those people who failed to take advantage of this opportunity could sometimes find themselves helped towards the well-intentioned and allegedly ameliorative process of institutionalised training. There appears to have been little discernible change in this situation during the sixties. In a late 1960s study limited to 17 to 20 year-old males, Martin Davies found that the majority of probation clients in that category lived their lives 'within the mainstream of affluence', although he did identify a significant minority who experienced material hardship (Davies, 1974).

It is not our intention to suggest that the probation client of the eighties is totally distinct in problem profile or offending pattern. Rather we suggest that the 'significant minority' of disadvantaged and more persistent offenders has increased. Furthermore, we do not claim that their level of disadvantage and deprivation is greater; that is relative and problematic as far as calculation is concerned. We simply suggest that there are now more people in this position, walking into probation offices with feelings of despair, frustration and anger and knocking on the enquiries hatch. We will explore the possible reasons for this later, but firstly let us juxtapose our claims (derived partly from listening to officers' impressionistic commentaries) with some data and observations of some of the researchers in this field.

David Haxby, in arguing for a 'correctionalist' service, was prescient in his description of an offender service with the primary task of developing a range of alternatives to custody, and consolidated within the penal system:

> This task will take it well beyond the provision of probation officers to 'advise, assist and befriend' offenders. It will have a responsibility to promote a range of services designed to assist in the rehabilitation of offenders and the prevention of recidivism. (Haxby, 1978, p. 90)

The language used here could have come straight from the government Green and White Papers preceding the 1991 Criminal Justice Act. Indeed, the vision put forward by Haxby was based on the experiences of the innovative alternative sentences of Community Service and Day Training. That the vision was becoming a reality was confirmed by Willis several years later:

> To the extent that probation officers were successful in displacing offenders from custody, they would now be using community based sentences for the more marginal and less tractable types of offender: the sort who would formerly have been sent down. (Willis, 1986)

Although it is implicit in Willis' observation, other writers have explicitly highlighted the effect of this trend on the nature of the relationship between probation workers and their clients, suggesting that as 'types of clients' alter, staff stress will increase and work practices will change (May, 1991). In other words, probation workers, particularly in field teams, are day to day dealing with more heavily convicted people with difficult social and personal problems, and within systems of greater accountability. There is evidence of the direction of this trend in some of the statistical information gathered by the Home Office. In respect of reports for court, for instance, the 1975 and 1991 volumes of 'Probation Statistics' show a dramatic decline in the number of reports prepared by the probation service for juveniles:

	Number	*Reports on juveniles as a percentage of all reports*
1974	56 646	26
1989	12 030	6

At the beginning of the eighties a significant proportion of those commencing supervision had no previous convictions. A proper concern about misdirected effort, injustice and unnecessary interference in people's life, aided by the introduction of information systems, prompted many services to monitor and reduce the numbers falling into this category (these figures are again drawn from Home Office 'Probation Statistics'):

	Probationers with no previous convictions (%)
1980	25
1989	13

A further indicator of the trend towards dealing with more persistent offenders is the percentage of those people placed on probation during the same period who had a previous custodial sentence:

	Probationers with previous custodial sentence
1980	22
1989	38

Another, though less striking, indicator has been the increase in people being supervised who have been convicted of a violent offence:

	Probationers convicted of violent offence (%)
1974	4.5
1989	11

So the trend is reasonably easy to identify, but the reasons for the trend are complicated and most certainly provide the basis for polemical debate both with the service and academic circles; they are worth some consideration.

The sources of change

The growth of 'alternatives to custody' has been seen as largely a regressive process, responsible for the dispersal of control into the community (Cohen, 1985). Although the 'Trojan Horse' metaphor has been rigorously and effectively challenged (Vass and Weston, 1990), alternatives to custody are still open to the charge that they served as a fulcrum for the lever that tilted the service towards correction. They certainly exposed probation staff to close proximity work with 'heavy end' offenders (hostels did likewise but were further from the mainstream of probation practice). Ironically, the ideological aversion of some officers to places like Day Centres may have enhanced the standard probation order as a rival alternative, thus ensuring its diminution as a welfare provision for the casualties of the criminal justice system. However, to isolate alternatives as the cause of the Service's shift towards working with higher risk offenders is too simplistic. There are a number of interlocking developments that we need to reflect on to arrive at a more complete picture.

(i)   The demise of institutional rehabilitation

As long as approved schools, borstals and prisons retained the aims of reforming and rehabilitating the people in them, the potential and the actual recidivist could be safely sent to them by the courts for a dose of discipline, work, school and moral influence (Mathiesen, 1990). Throughout this century there has been a growing recognition of the failure of such institutions to achieve either of these aims. This has led to the demise of approved schools and borstals (the latter to be reincarnated as a Young Offender Institution) and a besieged but nevertheless well-fed existence for the other. The 'fiasco' of prisons will no doubt continue, but the political problems caused by prison overcrowding have assisted the dispersal of rehabilitation from inside their walls into the community (Vanstone, 1993). The imperative of the Conservative Government of the eighties has been to shift rehabilitation, now wrapped in the rhetoric of punishment, from prison to the community for a significant number of offenders. This policy, as indicated in the last chapter, rests almost entirely on the probation service's willingness to move 'centre stage'.

(ii)   The birth of an after-care service

In 1963 the Advisory Council on the Treatment of Offenders recommended that the task of after-care, hitherto undertaken by the National Association of Discharged Prisoners Aid Societies, should be taken over by a larger probation service. This not only led to the seconding of probation officers to prisons but also to probation officers supervising in the community people who often had longer criminal careers than the average probationer. Within a relatively short period of time following the introduction of parole in the 1967 Criminal Justice Act, probation officers were supervising serious offenders within a tightly drawn framework of bureaucratic accountability (Coker, 1988; McWilliams, 1987). Perhaps clearer evidence of the kinds of work areas to which probation officers were being drawn (and before Community Service and Day Training Centres) was to be seen in specialist after-care units like those in Borough High Street in London, Manchester and Gloucester. These units were teams consisting of officers who specialised in exclusive work with the after-care and through-care of both voluntary and statutory prisoners. One of the authors worked in such unit in the early seventies and recalls the palpable wear and tear of the work on officers who were seconded for a maximum of two years.

(iii) Specialisation

After care was an early example of specialism, and as such at that time relatively rare. With growing diversification of practice locations, the number of officers working in specialisms grew until at the end of the eighties 48 per cent of serving probation officers had a specialism as their principal function (Davies and Wright, 1989). The extension of officers' work experience, and a concomitant expansion in skills and knowledge, were important developments, but the growth of specialist experience also widened the number of officers who experienced contact with more serious offenders as a normal part of their work.

(iv) The humanitarian motive

The movement towards dealing with more serious offenders in the community can be seen from one perspective as net-widening, and thus a contributory factor in the growing apparatus of state control (Cohen, 1985; Drakeford, 1983). It is also possible (although challengeable) that it is symptomatic of a long-term historical drift towards more humane and enlightened ways of dealing with transgressors, which transcends political ideology and temporary policy regressions. From this perspective a comparison of the penal policy of the late nineteenth century and the late twentieth century reveals a diminution of the infliction of pain. The probation service would naturally have a central place in a less painful and even pain-free penality.

(v) The imposition of purpose

The National Statement of Objectives and Priorities marked the beginning of the government's effort to consolidate the service as a provider of community-based alternatives to custody. In itself it was not a cause of the trend towards dealing with more serious offenders, but its significance should not be under-estimated. It started a process which has culminated in the 1991 Criminal Justice Act and had its roots in the Younger Report of 1974 which, although it had quite a different emphasis, promulgated the principle of punishment in the community through its proposal of 72-hour detention as part of a 'supervision and control' order.

To summarise the argument so far, we have suggested that since the 1960s a number of profound changes have impinged upon probation practice. Some of these (to be examined in more detail in Chapter 8) have been organisational, but in the day-to-day practice world there has been a clearly discernible change in the type of person being supervised by probation workers. We have identified some possible explanations of the complex processes which have produced this outcome. What we can still say with confidence is that probation workers continue to work with the disadvantaged and poor, among them a growing number of black people and women who suffer a double jeopardy of disadvantage and overt discrimination. The probation workers' point of intervention, however, has been hoisted up several notches so that the people they work with have a longer history of offending and experience of custody.

Case studies

We have so far addressed the question of who probation clients are in broad descriptive and more specifically statistical terms. To bring them to life, we now give a number of pen pictures of present-day probation clients. These are fictionalised accounts of real people, and represent aspects both of the plight of many people who fall foul of the criminal justice system and of the challenges to the modern probation practitioner.

Jim is an eighteen year old, the eldest of five children. His mother died when he was nine years old. Up until that time the family had lived a settled, fairly untroubled existence on a small council estate like many of those built during the sixties. His father remarried approximately eighteen months after his mother's death. Jim, never being able to accept his step-mother, rowed frequently with her, and his relationship with her and his father deteriorated. He began to miss school, sniffing glue and eventually using amphetamines and cannabis. Offences of taking and driving away, burglaries of shops and factories and shoplifting led to two periods in care. At the age of sixteen he was given a six-month YOI sentence for several burglaries. During the period when he was supervised by the probation service he committed further offences of burglary and theft and was given a Community Service Order and subsequently probation. Jim is bright and totally under-stimulated by government training schemes. He sees his drug-taking and offending as a rational response to his situation.

Chris is twenty-two years old and is one of four brothers all of whom have been in trouble with the police. He has six previous convictions for theft from vehicles, taking and driving away, and assault. He lives in a run-down neglected housing estate which is surrounded by well-to-do new housing developments. His father is an ex-miner who is disabled by a chronic chest condition and his mother is a very timid nervous woman. They are caring parents who are incapable of exercising control over their sons. Chris has already served two sentences of YOI and completed a Community Service Order and a programme at the service's day centre. He is co-operative with the probation service but shows little motivation to stop offending.

Carol is a twenty-six-year-old single parent who has seven previous convictions for theft from her employer, shoplifting and assault. She is currently on probation for a series of cheque frauds. Previous sentences have included prison, fines and community service. She did not offend until her late teens following the suicide of her father who had suffered from a manic-depressive illness. It is now known that she was sexually abused by her uncle during several years of her childhood. Her younger brother has appeared regularly before the courts but her older sister married and works as a nurse in a local hospital. Her relationship with her mother is at the same time dependent and volatile. Carol, who has a three-year-old daughter, is unemployed and reliant on state benefit; her debts and outgoings leave her with little disposable income. She has very low self-esteem and can be very manipulative. A self-acknowledged problem is her quick temper and aggressively defensive behaviour which is exacerbated by occasional bouts of heavy drinking.

David is a nineteen-year-old black male who has been subject to probation supervision on two previous occasions and has completed a twenty-month sentence at a young offender institution. He lives with his parents and two younger sisters in their own home on a large, sprawling council estate. Previous offences include robbery and burglary of business premises. He readily admits to offences that he has committed and co-operates with the probation service. However, he thinks that probation officers generally do not understand him or the full extent of the racism that he faces. Recently he served four months on remand for numerous cases of burglary which were subsequently thrown out of court; he received no compensation. Unemployed and constantly short of money, he is resigned to continued harassment and day-to-day survival on the streets.

Varieties of practice

The insight-giving casework approach (Biestek, 1961; Monger, 1972) seems remote from current probation practice, although the dearth of descriptive accounts of one-to-one work leaves the lingering suspicion that it survives as part of a box of techniques into which the modern probation officer still dips. But any attempt to describe what the probation service does with Jim, Chris, Carol and David inevitably focuses on a variety of innovations which are primarily group-work based and often stem from bottom-up initiatives which are sustained only for as long as the commitment, energy and enthusiasm of the workers concerned is sustained. A recent survey (Caddick, 1991) identified 1500 groupwork programmes and concluded that it was now more than a 'marginal activity'. The types of groups covered offending behaviour; life or social skills; alcohol education; activity; women; motoring offenders; sex offenders; temporary release; induction; drugs/addiction; control of anger and temper; and hostel residents. Their aims span a diverse range: supply of information; behaviour change; insight and understanding; empowerment; support and group action for wider change. Only three were found to have exclusively black membership, and women's groups particularly were seen to be the result of practitioner rather than management initiative. There are examples of work which is resourced and sustained through organisational commitment: for instance, work with sex offenders in Bristol (Weaver and Fox, 1984), and work based on a harm-reduction approach with problem drinkers (Doherty *et al.*, 1990). However, the practice literature of the past ten years also reveals projects which on the face of it appear to be carried by the practitioner with the support of the agency as opposed to carried by the agency and serviced by practitioners. Examples include an attempt to address the needs of black people through an informal reporting centre in Leeds (Pinder, 1982); the use of art in offence-focused work (Liebmann, 1991) and mediation work with victims and offenders (for example, Smith *et al.*, 1988). A good example of this category of project, which initially faltered but which was subsequently supported and sustained by the agency, is the Turas auto-crime project in Belfast (Chapman, 1992) and further examples are discussed in Chapter 7.

The emergent picture is of piecemeal innovations which provide stimulus and an area of autonomy for officers, a respite from the day-to-day routine of reports and court work, and possible value to the recipients. It seems true that 'a striking feature of the growth of the probation service has always been its *ad hoc*, pragmatic nature' (Blagg and Smith, 1989). Such innovation is often neutralised by the organisation until it withers and dies, or lingers on in the margins of the agency activity. New methods learned on courses are followed by an initial flurry of activity and resources, but the learning is dissipated in transfer to other tasks and situations (Ainley, 1979). It is not surprising, therefore, that with a few notable exceptions which will be examined in detail in Chapter 5, there is an absence of evaluation – a 'demonstrability gap'. This gap is a key reason for the transience of so much probation work. The lack of investment in research, which can provide the structure for and the expectation of continued commitment to practice initiatives, also ensures that the opportunity of achieving the components of a learning organisation is missed, and the full value of a great deal of pioneering work is lost. The history of one well-known approach provides an interesting illustration (cf. Smith, 1990).

Social skills

The 1980s have been called the 'age of Priestley and McGuire' and indeed the Social Skills and Personal Problem Solving approach advanced by them constitutes the most pervasive and positive influence on probation practice since the early 1970s (Priestley *et al.*, 1978). Its plethora of ideas, materials and exercises contained within a common-sense four-stage framework of assessment, objectives, learning and evaluation, combined with the endorsement of the client as collaborator in the action as opposed to passive recipient, satisfied the hunger of probation officers for optimism and tangible, usable methods. The late seventies and early eighties saw short courses on the approach proliferate, and a large number of programmes designed to meet a range of client needs followed. Complete day centre programmes were shaped by it (McGuire, 1978; Vanstone, 1986) along with a whole range of short group projects on subjects such as employment, violence, alcohol and welfare rights. Some of these, the Sheffield and Pontypridd Day Training Centres for example, were evaluated. Although one reviewer regards the arguments for the effectiveness of the approach as stronger than for analytic/therapeutic methods, she concludes that:

In view of the small number of research studies and their limited nature, the empirical case for social skills training for offenders is not a strong one. (Hudson, 1988)

She then gives a very accurate diagnosis of the reason for this, including the limitations of training, the lack of effective consultation and supervision, the superficiality of the pro- grammes, inappropriate group membership and the lack of outcome research. The problem in our view lies not in the Priestley and McGuire message, based as it was on collab- oration, a clear structure which included evaluation and systematic application of methods drawn from successful work in the field of psychology, but in the way it was received. The short course, which was the vehicle for delivering the message, was mistakenly perceived by some as a model for practice. This, combined with officers' satisfaction with having something new, interesting, enjoyable and stimulating to offer to hitherto dis- affected client groups, created a superficiality which reduced the potential impact of the approach and has resulted in the con- siderable efforts of officers and clients going largely un- catalogued and unevaluated.

Using research

Why is a service, made up of a large number of people committed to the idea of giving the poor and disadvantaged effective help and of reducing offending, so apparently uninterested in addressing questions such as 'Why are we doing this? What is this that we are doing? Is it having the intended effect?'. Why is a vast amount of potentially valuable work not evaluated or written up, or at best consigned to archive shelves? In order to answer these questions we have to explore issues of the use, or non-use, of research and information in the probation service.

The negative research findings of the 1970s have been well documented and do not need repeating in detail here (Gendreau and Ross, 1979; Raynor, 1985; Vass, 1990): the received message, however mistaken, was that nothing works. Ironically, then and subsequently, practitioners have continued to show different ways of living with the research results; the social skills approach, for instance, is rehabilitative and reformative in intent. What the research did do was widen the chasm between research and practice, and influence policy towards a concentration on diversion. Practitioners, meanwhile, whilst in the middle of a polemic which argued that they were either wasting their time or oppressing the poor, continued to deal with the day-to-day realities of the criminal justice system. Sustained either by stoicism or a continuing commitment to what they were doing, or a mixture of both, probation workers continued to pursue a rehabilitative and reformative approach in both one-to-one and group work. It is at an organisational and policy level that the influence of research findings can be discerned: the growth of diversion from custody and of justice and proportionality as dominant ideals is evidence of that. Success in keeping someone out of custody or in delaying their entry into the system offered much more tangible evidence of effectiveness, as newly defined, than was available from direct work with clients.

If the negative experience of engaging with research is one reason for a lack of critical curiosity within the service, attitudes towards research and the relationship between practitioners and researchers provide further insight into the problem. The argument that research transactions are, firstly, one-sided exploitative ones, in which the workers are damned and the researchers assume all the glory, and, secondly, the exclusive property of academic experts, because they are based on empiricism, has been attacked as an example of defensiveness in the face of negative findings and of an over-reliance on 'quasi-anthropological or ethno-methodological methods' (Sheldon, 1984, commenting on Raynor, 1984). However, engaging in discussion with practitioners about research can reveal the counterproductive persuasiveness of the positivist argument.

Workers are inclined to say, 'If you can't set up a "proper" controlled experiment (and usually you can't) then the enterprise is doomed from the start' (Smith, 1987). Such a stance effectively rules out any kind of practitioner research. What is the point, it might be asked, of asking people if they have been helped, if their subjective replies will not survive the rigour of positivist research criteria? In the face of such a lack of confidence about following the path of curiosity, intuition seems as good as anything else.

The satisfying of curiosity requires some form of information. A recent analysis of the attitudes of probation staff to information provides some interesting clues to the service's difficulty in using and evaluating information (Humphrey and Pease, 1992). The researchers found that the majority of staff of all grades when talking about effectiveness talk in terms of input. In other words, they define effectiveness in terms of how many people were diverted from custody or how many appropriate orders were made by the courts. They talk less about the impact of their work on people's problems or offending, and survive by holding on to 'an act of faith in the validity of their intervention, no matter how restricted their role may have become'. As for information itself, the 'troops' see this as something required by a management within an organisation which is becoming increasingly bureaucratic. The result is that information systems which have the potential of underpinning a critical culture in the service have the unintended consequence of hardening the negative attitudes of practitioners to 'research activity'. A more suggestive and optimistic finding of the research, however, was that officers who can be described as 'believers' in what they are doing are more ready to discuss their work and its effectiveness. They might be the key to an offender-centred strategy implemented by curious practitioners.

Conclusion

The service faces some very real challenges and difficult problems. However, there already exists a practice base which is underpinned by the principle of offering relevant help to people to reduce their offending within a collaborative relationship. There is abundant evidence of energy, ideas and innovative practice in the service. The challenge is around the issue of how that creativity can be harnessed to produce a confident service, not bedevilled by the care versus control dilemma, and clear about its intent and its effectiveness. The problems are inter-related and multiple, but resolvable; the rest of the book is an attempt to explore how they might be resolved. The main issues can be summarised here.

Probation officers work within a criminal justice system which discriminates against black people and women, in particular. Awareness of this has increased during recent years, particularly because of a series of research findings and the attention of a number of pressure groups within and outside the National Association of Probation Officers. The addressing of equal opportunities policies is in place in most probation areas; converting statements of intent into practical action is another matter. Indeed, the permeation of every sphere of probation activity with an anti-discriminatory perspective is still some way off. It will depend on the service's ability to act effectively as a pressure group within the system whilst at the same time challenging its own policies and practices. While training is essential to this, its effect will be neutralised without increased numbers of black staff and a commitment throughout the organisation to developing an anti-racist culture.

There is an imperative to create a model of practice, based on evidence, which survives changes in personnel and fashions. This will necessitate a fusion of practice and research and an heuristic approach to work within an organisational culture in which all members of staff seek critical feedback on their performance, so that evaluation is properly resourced and recognised as both a legitimate activity of probation staff and a crucial element in improved practice. Information systems will need to be uncoupled from management systems so that they are no longer seem as devices to 'screw people down' but rather as the essential prerequisite to satisfied curiosity. It follows that management needs to be freed from the shackles of the 'right to manage' and macho principles of the Thatcher years and to adopt a style more relevant to the needs of an organisation whose business is people not products.

During the eighties and early nineties the service has been adjusting its report writing and court intervention work away from the ideology of treatment and towards the principle of diverting people from custody through community-based alternatives. It is now faced with, on the one hand, research findings which suggest that some interventions can be effective in reducing offending and, on the other hand, with a Criminal Justice Act which on the face of it eliminates the 'risk of custody' focus and supplants it with just deserts principles which embroil probation officers in assessments of the seriousness of offences. Maintaining an individualised approach to understanding offending and how it can be addressed, which is compatible with a rational approach to 'just deserts' sentencing, will depend on a thorough rethink of report-writing practice.

The service, despite the process of change taking place, will continue to work primarily with individuals and their offending and their problems – that much will not change. Given that people's actions take place within the context of social problems and differential levels of choice and opportunity, the probation service will need to reconcile the task of assisting the rehabilitation of individual people with the need for change in the structural problems of unemployment, poor housing and poverty. This is by no means a new dilemma but it is assuming a growing relevance.

3

Influencing Sentencers: Just Deserts and System Strategies

Introduction

The aim of this chapter is to show how thinking and practice in pre-sentence report writing have developed since the early 1970s. From 1975 on, social enquiry reports, as they were then called, came under attack on both theoretical and empirical grounds, to the point where it became impossible to defend traditional models of practice. There were even suggestions that these reports should be abandoned altogether. Other writers, however, argued for a new rationale for reports which rejected the discredited 'treatment model' but still allowed for sentences to be individualised by taking into account the offender's circumstances; the new model also encouraged thinking about pre-sentence reports as a means of influencing the working of local criminal justice systems. Developments in juvenile justice in the 1980s, which both affected and reflected changes in legislation, suggested more grounds for optimism about the role of such reports, both in influencing sentencers and in providing a starting-point for relevant and appropriate forms of practice with people on probation. While practice remains uneven, and the messages of the 1980s have still not been heeded as much as they might have been, there are good grounds for believing that pre-sentence reports in the early 1990s are generally better, in quite specific ways, than they were ten years earlier. First, however, a cautionary note.

How not to write pre-sentence reports

Early in 1989 one of us completed a research report on community-based provision for young adult offenders in a deprived area in Scotland. Part of the research entailed a content analysis of a sample of pre-sentence reports (still called social enquiry reports in Scotland) prepared for a particular Sheriff Court, which had better remain nameless. While there were substantial variations in the quality of reports between individual social workers and district offices, many were judged to contain such faults as to make them more suitable as awful warnings to students than as aids to sentencers in making decisions. If so, they will not have been written in vain.

Five kinds of problem were identified in these reports: technical failings, negative and moralistic judgements, circumlocution, irrelevant content, and conclusions which were vague or contradictory. The first included errors of spelling or grammar, which may have been mainly attributable to the haste with which reports were written and typed, in which case sentencers might understand and forgive. But some mistakes (such as mis-spelling the name of the court) suggested lack of care rather than lack of time; and others suggested lack of thought. For example, one report opened, as was common, with a long list of the defendant's near relatives, giving their relationship to him, their age and whereabouts. One sister was listed as 'probably in Hartlepool' and, while the father's age was said to be 'not known', his 'present status' was given as 'deceased'. This was an extreme case, but it was not unusual to read phrases which had clearly undergone some unwanted transformation between the writer's thought and its expression on the page. For example, to say that 'patterns of behaviour were

numerous' is true of all of us, but not helpful; a report writer has
an obligation to notice when a crucial word has gone missing.

When writers on social work say, as they still sometimes do,
that social workers should be 'non-judgemental', what they
usually mean, and ought to mean, is that they should avoid making
judgements which are crudely moralistic, negative and stereo-
typing. In the sample in question, this kind of judgement was
common; the following quotations give a flavour of what was said:

> It did not take D too long to make his first of many appear-
> ances at the Sheriff Court ... His overview of this offence is
> filtered by low morality and lack of insight; D says little to
> indicate any truthful regret, except that he was caught ... he
> has great control and determination.

> Offending, unfortunately, has been the main feature of her life
> thus far ... [She] has few interests outside of drinking and
> gaming machines ... she appears prematurely hardened to such
> a way of life.

> I was struck by his distorted and senseless view of morality.

> The writer has observed tendencies to deceit.

(In the last quotation, it is presumably the writer who has done
the observing, and the defendant who has the tendencies.)
Judgements of this kind were often associated with veiled or
open suggestions that a custodial sentence would be appropriate;
but even when they were not, they inevitably undermined any
suggestion at the end of the report that a community sentence
might be feasible.

Such negative character assessments were sometimes wrapped
up in a peculiar jargon, made up in part of words and phrases
drawn from legal or social scientific discourses (as noted by
Horsley (1984)), but also used for purposes of euphemism, when
the writer wished to express a negative opinion, but felt unable to
do so in plain language. The following (admittedly extreme)
example perhaps contains elements of all of these:

Should such problems arise again, the writer would suggest respectfully a specialist in emotional/mental life be used for assessment if the court is disposed to do so at present ... She knows she can seek voluntary help. Otherwise regretfully the writer has no positive recommendation to make in this instance, other than to add a disposal which is not immediate or requires co-operation with the concomitant enforcement for non-compliance is unlikely to be successful.

The first sentence eludes understanding altogether (a 'not' missing, perhaps?), but the second, being interpreted, means 'send her down', which is what the court did. It should not be necessary to labour the point that reports should be written in clear, straightforward language, but in some places at least it may be.

Many reports in this sample contained material whose relevance to the offence was obscure to say the least. In this they showed the importance of the emphasis on relevance of content (now restated in national standards for both Scotland, and England and Wales) in the practice guidelines produced by the Home Office (1986) and the Department of Health and Social Security (1987), which themselves reflected growing academic and practice-based criticism of what could be called the 'kitchen sink' school of report-writing – that is, the belief that everything is potentially relevant and should be thrown in (Raynor, 1980; 1985; Thorpe et al., 1980). The irrelevancies in the sample reports were of two main kinds. Firstly, an inordinate amount of space was often devoted to the defendant's history in care; this material was presumably drawn from old files which included a record of movement between placements, which was often given in great and confusing detail. (Probation officers would have had the advantage of not having such records to hand.) Secondly, there was often a lengthy history of the defendant's family relationships, going back to early childhood, even when these had not been problematic enough to lead to social work inter-vention. A corollary of these preoccupations was that in many reports the circumstances of the offence itself received barely a mention, although it was, of course, the fact that an offence had been committed which led to the report in the first place. There was also often a lack of specificity about what previous social work interventions had actually consisted of, or been intended to achieve; very broad aims like 'rehabilitation' and 'support' were mentioned, usually in the context of explaining why there was no point in trying anything more, although previous social work seemed to have focused on the issue of offending in only a very few cases.

Finally, there were problems in the conclusions of many reports. A few were straightforward invitations to impose a custodial sentence: 'a custodial sentence is the only sentence that would satisfy the court' is a statement with a strong self-fulfilling potential. Others conveyed the same message indirectly. A larger number, however, concluded with some argument in favour of a non-custodial measure, but this tended to be made in a way which did not suggest much optimism about the outcome. Probation might be suggested, for example, followed by a gloomy prediction of the likelihood of its being breached, a statement of the defendant's own view that 'a jail sentence would do him a world of good', or doubts about the defendant's motivation and commitment. Even when a community measure was proposed without these qualifications, the envisaged content and focus of the order were rarely made explicit, perhaps because the lack of an offence focus in the report meant that the writer had no clear idea what the purpose of the order might be, or because of lack of confidence, or lack of resources. In fact, there were good facilities in the area for work on substance abuse, but they were mentioned as a resource in only three out of 70 reports, despite the high frequency with which drink and drug problems were said to feature in defendants' lives. There was only rarely a sense that probation could achieve a relevant focus on offending or on related problems such as substance abuse, or provide an opportunity for positive learning and development.

It seems worth stressing the shortcomings of the reports in this sample, because it is common to hear that the court reports of the late 1980s bore no resemblance to the products of the early years of the decade. At least in this area, in 1988, this was not true. Readers in England and Wales may feel that these problems reflect specifically Scottish circumstances, and that low standards are only to be expected in a country without a probation service; but, while we have been assured by probation officers for some years that 'we all do offence-focused reports now', impressionistic evidence and accounts from practitioners of what this actually means suggests that practice is still widely divergent between areas, offices and individuals. We are certainly not suggesting that nothing in pre-sentence report practice changed during the 1980s; we believe that it did, and in the right direction, and we discuss these developments in the next section. We do argue, however, that there is no room for complacency; and a National Standard in itself provides no guarantee of high quality, although it may help to fix a minimum baseline.

Pre-sentence reports in the 1970s

The publication of Bottoms and McWilliams' (1979) article on a 'non-treatment paradigm' for probation crystallised for many practitioners and commentators their growing unease about the theoretical basis of much probation practice. The 1960s and 1970s had seen the probation service undergo a dramatic expansion, not least in its role as provider of information to the courts through the medium of social inquiry reports (SIRs). By the end of this period, however, both the theoretical justification and the empirical effect of all this effort were being questioned. At the theoretical level, it had become impossible for most probation officers to continue to defend the notion that SIRs could provide either an accurate, impartial diagnosis of the nature of a defendant's 'illness', or a scientific prognosis of the likely effect of any 'treatment' the court might impose. The 'medical model' of offending, which in extreme versions literally viewed it as the symptom of an illness (Winnicott, 1962), had been substantially discredited by new currents in criminological thought which emphasised the element of choice (albeit often under constraints) in the commission of crime. Offenders, by and large, could have chosen not to offend; crime, unlike acne, could not be seen as an involuntary symptom of disease.

The theoretical discredit was reinforced by empirical evidence that appeared to say that whatever it was that probation officers did when they supervised offenders on probation, it did not have the effect of 'curing' them of offending (Folkard *et al.*, 1976). In relation to SIRs particularly, the work of Perry (1974) and Thorpe (1979) revealed inconsistencies in length, format, and the type of information included in reports, findings which hardly supported the image of probation officers as a homogeneous body of scientific experts dispassionately advising sentencers. And while some studies (Mott, 1977; Hine *et al.*, 1978) suggested that magistrates' thinking was influenced by reports, particularly by their conclusions, there was no evidence that this influence worked in a consistent direction – for example, to reduce the use of custody (although a suggestion of custody in an SIR was a strong predictor of a custodial sentence). Rather, the effect seemed to be to change the distribution of non-custodial sentences, increasing the use of probation, for instance, at the expense not of custody but of fines (Curran, 1983). Recent work suggests that this is still the case, at least in Crown Courts (Moxon, 1988; Raynor, 1991). Finally, there was no evidence to sustain the hope that an increase in SIR provision would lead to an improvement in the overall quality of sentencing, measured by the level of reconviction after any given sentence, or to greater consistency of sentencing practice (Tarling, 1979), both of which should have occurred if probation officers really had the expertise and influence they sometimes claimed.

The Streatfeild Report (Home Office, 1961), which contained what was for perhaps twenty years the single most influential statement available on the content and purposes of reports, had appeared at the high tide of rehabilitative optimism; and with the ebbing of the tide, it seemed as if the justification for having SIRs at all might have disappeared. One response (Perry, 1974; Herbert and Mathieson, 1975) to this discomfort was to argue that reports could be improved by including more information, assembled from a standard list much longer than anything proposed by Streatfeild (Herbert and Mathieson were particularly strong advocates of the 'kitchen sink' approach; reports prepared on their plan would have been of epic length). Another, ultimately more influential, response was to argue that reports should become more focused in content and that writers should be clearer about their purposes. One of the present writers (Raynor, 1980) argued that even were sentencing practice to abandon any concern with individualised treatment and move towards 'just deserts' as the basis for sentencing decisions, there would still be a place for SIRs, since it would still be desirable to individualise sentences – no longer on grounds of a need for treatment, but on those of culpability or blameworthiness.

Making sense of reports

Unlike some later writers (Tutt and Giller, 1984), Raynor continued to see the SIR as a social work document – that is, as one informed by values such as care and respect for persons, drawing on social work skills in its preparation, and representing a distinctive contribution to the decision-making process. Thus, while Tutt and Giller's position (at least for juvenile courts) was that report writers should always argue for the 'least restrictive sanction', Raynor argued that the report could form a basis for a negotiated contract between the defendant, the probation service (or another social work agency) and the court. One point of difference is that Raynor took a rather more optimistic view than Tutt and Giller of the potential value of social work intervention. Tutt and Giller's argument was heavily influenced by the then new 'systemic' thinking about juvenile justice, which tended (on the basis of the 1970s 'effectiveness' research) to scepticism about the value of any intervention, which was seen as more likely to be damaging than helpful, by labelling the offender as in need of some form of help and then failing to provide it, and by increasing the chances of a more severe penalty on any subsequent court appearance. It was therefore better to avoid it.

Minimal intervention was therefore in the defendant's best interests, and the report writer's principal aim should be to keep offenders 'down tariff' for as long as possible.

As Bottoms and Stelman (1988) note, a difficulty with this position is that it makes the SIR in effect indistinguishable from the defence plea of mitigation, since this too is likely to seek the lowest possible sentence; and Tutt and Giller assumed that the report should consider all the issues which might be relevant to sentencing, such as the need to protect the public or considerations of general deterrence, rather than those which are specifically the province of a social work agency. Although it had become customary by the late 1970s to speak of the concluding comments in SIRs as 'recommendations', Raynor (1980), following the Streatfeild Committee in this, argued that the term was inappropriate, since it suggested 'an expertly selected treatment based on a scientific diagnosis'. Streatfeild had preferred the term 'opinion', and stressed that this should not be given in a form which implied that the writer was taking into account all the considerations before the court. Raynor suggested that instead of 'recommendations' we should think in terms of 'offers' of plausible alternatives to retributive sentencing; Bottoms and Stelman preferred the term 'suggestions' of non-custodial penalties; and this, as we shall see, is close to what is in fact envisaged under the 1991 Criminal Justice Act.

Like Tutt and Giller, Raynor considered that a defendant's tariff position, or place within the criminal justice system, was a relevant issue for the report writer, but allowed much more scope within this for sentences to be individualised. The basis for this, however, would be the offender's degree of moral blameworthiness; as, in judging people's actions in everyday life, we routinely take account of the circumstances in which they found themselves before coming to a conclusion, so the formal criminal justice system should allow us to consider the circumstances of an offence and whether these count as mitigating or aggravating factors. Mitigation on this basis is widely recognised as reasonable and on occasions demonstrated in practice, as when, for example, racist provocation is viewed as mitigating the seriousness of an assault, or a woman who has endured a history of violence from her partner is not sent to prison for killing him. Similarly, evidence of calculation or recklessness of others' welfare may reasonably count as aggravating the seriousness of a given offence. Thus, contrary to what was argued by proponents of the 'back to justice' position in the early 1980s, individualisation of sentencing need not be abandoned along with the treatment model; it has a longer history, and can outlive the demise of the 'rehabilitative ideal' (Raynor, 1985). As we saw in Chapter 1, the 'just deserts' emphasis of the 1991 Act does not exclude this type of individualisation, and indeed allows factors unrelated to the offence to count as mitigation.

Legislation and pre-sentence reports

The 1982 Criminal Justice Act was a milestone in recent developments, since it specifically aimed to encourage the use of SIRs as a means of reducing the use of custody for young offenders. Section 1 of the Act greatly widened the statutory basis of reports by providing that a court could not pass a custodial sentence on anyone under the age of 21 without first considering a report, unless it believed that such a report was unnecessary. To dispense with a report one of three criteria had to be satisfied: that the offence was so serious that a non-custodial sentence could not be justified; that the protection of the public from serious harm demanded a custodial sentence; or that the offender was unable or unwilling to respond to a non-custodial measure. The Act was clear (in Section 2) that courts would normally need a report to determine whether any of these criteria were met. These provisions were strengthened in the 1988 Criminal Justice Act, which specified that the public protection criterion applied to serious harm from the defendant, thus disallowing the use of custody on exemplary or general deterrent grounds, and that there had to be a history of failure to respond to non-custodial measures before this criterion could be used.

When imposing a custodial sentence, courts were required to state in ordinary language which of the three criteria they felt were satisfied.

The 1991 Criminal Justice Act (Section 3) follows the logic of its predecessors in extending the general requirement to consider a pre-sentence report to all offenders, not only those under 21. The old criteria for custody are modified to lay greater stress on the seriousness of the offence; the protection of the public from harm is to be a consideration only with violent or sexual offences; and the criterion of chronic inability or unwillingness to respond to a non-custodial penalty is replaced by refusal of consent to a community penalty. The thrust of the sections of the 1991 Act which relate to sentencing is that the primary basis for decisions should be an assessment of the offender's 'just deserts'; the seriousness of the current offence should be the main ground for sentencing. It thus becomes clearly relevant for the pre-sentence report to contain information which will help the court reach a decision about the seriousness of the offence, much as envisaged by Raynor (1980). At the same time, although seriousness should determine the sentencing 'band' appropriate for the offender (discharges or monetary penalties; community sentences; custody), and the degree of restriction of liberty within that band, the Act allows for consideration of individual circumstances when a decision is being made about which type of sentence (for example, community service or some form of probation) would be most suitable. In this way, what Bottoms and Stelman (1988) call 'forward-looking' consider-ations, relevant to an offender's needs, the risks to which he or she is subject, and the resources available, can be reintroduced; and the pre-sentence report is pre-eminently the means by which these individual factors can be conveyed to the court.

The effect of the 1980s legislation on social inquiry report practice, coupled with practitioners' growing awareness that old habits needed to be changed, was undoubtedly to encourage greater specificity of content and a clearer view of purpose; as Tutt and Giller (1984) noted, the 1982 Act had the effect of concentrating the minds of report writers on concrete issues, such as a defendant's ability or willingness to respond to a particular non-custodial measure, rather than on more diffuse factors such as the possible criminogenic effect of (say) sibling rivalry. In the next section we draw on the experience of the 1980s in juvenile justice, which we outlined briefly in Chapter 1, to argue that developments in report writing practice formed a part of a successful wider strategy of 'system management'. Success stories are not a prominent feature of social work's recent history, so it is pleasant to be able to tell one.

Juvenile justice in the 1980s

The 1982 Act was generally greeted with foreboding by social workers concerned with offenders. In its reassertion of retributive punishment as a valid aim of the juvenile as well as the adult criminal justice system (most publicly identifiable in the 'short sharp shock' detention centre regime), its scepticism about treatment (shown, for example, in the abolition of borstal training), and its increase of the powers of sentencers (in respect of care orders) at the expense of those of social workers, it appeared to mark a decisive move away from the welfare emphasis which had characterised juvenile justice legislation for most of the twentieth century. Certainly this was how it was presented politically, as a major break with the supposed liberalism of the 1969 Children and Young Persons Act. In the prevailing gloom, few noticed (or took seriously) the fact that the 1982 Act also contained the first attempt to restrict sentencers' discretion by legislation, or considered that the failures of the 1969 Act perhaps demanded a radically new approach.

In January 1983 the Department of Health and Social Security announced, in Local Authority Circular 83(3), that £15 million would be made available to voluntary organisations to provide intermediate treatment facilities. The circular sought to encourage a shift in the balance of intermediate treatment provision away from low-key preventive work: priority would be given to proposals for intensive community-based services aimed at young offenders at risk of care or custody (Bottoms *et al.*, 1990). It was envisaged that local authorities would work in partnership with the voluntary organisations which received the funding, and that projects established would eventually (usually after three years) be absorbed into mainstream local authority provision. Local inter-agency liaison was thus seen as a central requirement, and it was hoped that the provision of 'bridging' funds would allow services in the community to be set up before the closure of residential establishments, enabling a transfer of resources from the residential sector to the community.

The initiative was carefully monitored by NACRO, whose final report (NACRO, 1991a) found that of 110 projects originally funded, only 15 had ceased to exist in any recognisable form. The arrangements proposed in Circular LAC 83(3) had proved workable, and NACRO's monitoring suggested that projects had in general succeeded in providing services for their intended target groups. Over roughly the same period, there was a dramatic decline (63 per cent between 1985 and 1989) in the use of custody for juveniles, and the effective disappearance of the criminal care order (formally abolished by the 1991 Act). The gloomy predictions which greeted the Act, and the findings of some early research (Burney, 1985) proved not to be borne out by events in juvenile justice (and although changes in the adult system were much less consistently encouraging, the trend from 1985 onwards was in the same direction (Barclay, 1991)). By the end of the 1980s developments in juvenile justice were widely regarded as representing a success for practice and policy, not least by the Home Office (1988), which specifically argued that lessons from the experience of intensive intermediate treatment should be drawn by the probation service for the adult sector. We therefore have to ask the unaccustomed question: what went right?

It would be too simple to attribute the success solely to the projects established by the 1983 initiative: for one thing, the use of custody for juveniles was declining from its 1981 peak before the first projects began their work. Other factors were undoubtedly important, including demographic changes: the overall number of juveniles available to be processed by the criminal justice system declined by about 25 per cent in the course of the 1980s (Pratt, 1985). As we suggested above, the 1982 Act's criteria for custody, as interpreted by courts and social workers (including probation officers), are likely to have had a helpful effect, along with its introduction of new forms of high tariff supervisory orders, which encouraged the provision of new non-custodial programmes, and new ways of suggesting their use in SIRs. In the new legislative context, specialist practitioners developed knowledge, skills and experience which they used with a confidence and sophistication rare in recent social work practice. Influenced by the advocacy of minimum intervention, workers also began to explore the strategic use of SIRs as a means of keeping offenders 'down tariff', for example, by suggesting repeated conditional discharges, perhaps backed by voluntary contact with the young offender, or trying to ensure that the more intensive forms of supervision were used only as a last resort.

Cautioning

Another important development was the consistent official encouragement during the 1980s of cautioning as the preferred means of dealing with juvenile offenders. The Home Office (1980) had early adopted a strong version of labelling theory's counter-intuitive prediction that a court appearance would increase, not reduce, the likelihood of subsequent offending, and was therefore to be avoided if possible. This advice was re-inforced by Circulars in 1985 and again in 1990 advocating increased use of cautioning, greater consistency of practice between police forces, and (in the second circular) more use of cautions for adults. While Evans and Wilkinson (1990) suggested that the 1985 circular had little specific effect, the use of cautions was rising before it and continued to rise after it. By 1989 73 per cent of known juvenile offenders received formal cautions (Barclay, 1991), compared with under 50 per cent ten years previously. Cautioning of adults only showed a substantial increase from 1986, and the rates remain much lower than for juveniles, at 19 per cent for 17–20 years-old and 16 per cent for those over 21. The disparity between 16 and 17 year-olds' chances of receiving a caution has seemed anomalous to many; one explanation offered is that 17 year-olds are less likely to be first offenders. This is true, but hardly adequate: Evans (1991) found that one-third of male 17–20 year-olds were first offenders, and two-thirds of females; a substantial proportion were therefore 'cautionable', if the criteria used with juveniles were applied. The 1991 Criminal Justice Act, which brings 16 and 17 year-olds together in a new legal category of 'youth', reflects a wish to make the system's response to 17 year-olds resemble the treatment of 16 year-olds; the risk is that instead of 17 year-olds being brought 'down' the system, 16 year-olds may be brought 'up'; but, given current trends in cautioning, this seems unlikely in respect of diversion from prosecution. It makes penological sense to caution a 17 year-old first-time offender, since s/he is statistically less likely to re-offend than a 14 year-old first timer.

Offence-focused practice and system management

The final element in the social work contribution to juvenile justice in the 1980s was the development of forms of practice with young offenders which focused on their offending and the circumstances surrounding it. Not only in the LAC 83(3) projects, but in specialist teams in social services departments and probation services, well-defined, highly structured programmes were developed which promised a guaranteed amount of contact with offenders on supervision. Magistrates were kept informed of offenders' progress, and guarantees were given that appropriate action would be taken in the event of a breach of the order's conditions. In this context, practitioners built upon the early ideas on the 'correctional curriculum' of Thorpe *et al.* (1980) to develop methods of work which were typically cognitively oriented, relevant to offenders' own perception of their situation, and offence-focused. The work of Denman (1982) was probably the single most influential source of ideas on practice, including some work in probation day centres, though it should be said that its potential as a basis for work with adult offenders was never fully exploited, unlike the social skills and personal problem-solving approach of Priestley *et al.* (1978). Like Priestley and his colleagues, Denman drew on work in cognitive psychology, especially the theory of personal constructs and the 'theory of reasoned action' (Riley and Tuck, 1986), to provide practical guidelines for social workers; it is a good (and rare) example of the use of theories from another discipline to inform social work practice. In its cognitive emphasis, its focus on offending, and its flexibility, which allowed other relevant problems to be addressed in a 'correctional' setting, Denman's work has affinities with the 'reasoning and rehabilitation' model discussed in Chapter 6.

There were, then, several strands to the practice which developed in the 1980s under the confusing label of 'inter-mediate treatment'. It united a commitment to relevant face-to-face work with offenders and a concern with the strategic management of the system as a whole. Hence, alongside the range of direct services which were developed, from minimal supervision to intensive and highly structured centre-based programmes, workers were involved in attempts to divert young offenders from prosecution through advocacy of cautions in inter-agency panels. Once offenders had been prosecuted, SIRs were used as a means of trying to lengthen the tariff 'ladder' at the bottom end, as well as of offering acceptable forms of community-based supervision at the top. NACRO's (1991a) monitoring of the centrally funded projects suggests that they were generally successful in working with the right group – persistent or relatively serious offenders for whom custody was a real risk. There is some evidence that this can also be achieved with intensive programmes for adult offenders (Raynor, 1988; Roberts, 1989), although the overall experience of top end 'alternatives to custody' is not altogether encouraging; it has been notoriously hard to ensure that they operate as alternatives to custody and not as alternatives to something else (Vass, 1990). Whatever the theoretical virtues of low tariff SIRs, however, the probation service has, since the Statement of National Objectives and Priorities (Home Office, 1984), been enjoined to concentrate SIRs on relatively high tariff offenders, and this tendency will be reinforced by the 1991 Act's demand for more reports in cases where the court is considering whether the criteria for custody are satisfied. The message of the 1980s' experience of juvenile justice remains: that it is essential to combine relevant and focused practice with individuals with a sensitive, critical awareness of the operations of the local criminal justice system as a whole.

Influencing sentencers in the 1990s

It is clear that the 1991 Act establishes a new context for pre-sentence report writing. More reports will have to be prepared, especially in Crown Courts, and more will have to be prepared quickly, to minimise delays in sentencing. The Act requires a PSR to be considered before a custodial sentence (normally), and before any of the more restrictive community sentences, including community service and probation orders with additional requirements. While the Act itself merely defines a PSR as a report in writing by a probation officer or local authority social worker, it also has implications for the content of reports. In particular, the Act's stress on the seriousness of the current offence as the basis for sentencing entails that PSRs should contain information relevant to a judgement about seriousness (mitigating or aggravating factors), and, in the case of violent or sexual offences, information relevant to a judgement about the risk to the public of serious harm.

In some respects, therefore, the new expectations of PSRs are wider than before, since material relating to the protection of the public can explicitly be included; in other respects they are narrower, following the trend in the 1980s towards greater specificity and focus; the training material produced by the

Home Office on PSRs is clear that information about the offender should only be included if it is demonstrably relevant – to past offending or past experience of the criminal justice system, to the likelihood of re-offending, or to a proposed community sentence. The suggested format for PSRs is an introduction, with a standard 'headline' paragraph, basic facts about the offender, and sources of information; an analysis of the current offence(s); relevant information about the offender; and a conclusion which should, except in very serious or trivial cases, consider one or more possible community sentences, including the degree of restriction of liberty each would entail. It remains legitimate to refer to the possible adverse effects of custody, and to give an opinion on which of the available community sentences would be most suitable.

It should be clear by now that much of what is proposed for PSRs is close to what we have identified as good practice as it emerged during the 1980s. The main differences are probably that the Act will require still closer attention to factors affecting the seriousness of offences and still greater clarity about what any community sentence would mean in practice. PSR writers will need to attend closely to the nature of offences, the characteristics of victims, and a range of potentially mitigating and aggravating factors such as premeditation, provocation, racial motivation, degree of pressure on the offender, his or her part in the offence, and so on. The Act also allows mitigation for reasons unrelated to the offence, such as youth or age, previous good character (or present good conduct in another aspect of life), and evidence of willingness to reform or seek appropriate help. Having assessed the seriousness of the offence in the light of such factors, the PSR writer will then need to analyse possible community sentences in terms of their restrictions on liberty (the essence of punishment as conceived in the Act) as well as of their suitability for the offender (need or otherwise for social work intervention, likelihood of successful completion, risk of reoffending, etc.).

If it is true that a good PSR will closely resemble a good SIR, it is possible to be optimistic about the ability of the probation service to influence sentencers in future. Indeed, as we have seen, the nature and purpose of PSRs as envisaged by the Home Office is close to what critics of traditional SIR practice have advocated. Fears of an exaggeratedly rigid format for PSRs, which would have been welcomed neither by probation officers nor by sentencers, have proved unfounded. There is still scope for individualisation of sentences under the Act, despite the apparent rigidity of 'just deserts'; and it takes further the tenor of earlier legislation, in seeing the PSR as a means of encouraging courts to consider community penalties. Individual considerations are to operate both at the stage of judging seriousness and, where relevant, at that of choosing between community penalties, now firmly identified as sentences and situated within the just deserts framework (Bottoms, 1989). There is thus still room for the values of social work in PSR practice; and while, in areas where the 'kitchen sink' approach is still favoured, it will no doubt take both PSR writers and sentencers time to adjust, the presence of a National Standard should help the process. The next chapter looks more closely at issues of quality in PSR preparation, and in particular advocates a process of team auditing which should help to improve and maintain standards more effectively than a national statement, and to promote a practical approach to anti-discriminatory practice in this field.

4

Consistency and Quality in Pre-Sentence Reports

Introduction: pre-sentence reports, justice and discrimination

The juvenile justice research and practice of the 1980s showed, as outlined in the last chapter, not only the harm which can result from poor social inquiry practice but some of the benefits which improvement can bring. This chapter explores these issues further in the new context of pre-sentence reports and the 1991 Act, and considers ways in which the challenges posed by the research can be met. The issue is not simply one of good professional practice: when reports are poorly prepared, inconsistent in quality, unreliable in their conclusions or illogical or poorly targeted in their proposals, one of the first casualties is justice. The new sentencing framework aims at more consistent justice; this chapter will review some of the evidence about the PSR's potential contribution to this, and suggest how probation officers and their managers might work together to make the impact of PSRs both fairer and more effective. As long ago as 1976 it was suggested ironically that one of the most important decisions offenders could make was to choose their report writers carefully (Bean, 1976), and while probation officers continue to complain of inconsistent sentencing by the courts they will surely wish to address those aspects of inconsistency which lie within their direct control.

As the previous chapter showed, this is not simply a matter of recommendations or proposals, but also of general content. These take on a particular significance in the context of reports on people who are already disadvantaged or exposed to differential treatment in their contacts with the criminal justice system. A tendency to recommend probation proportionately less often for black clients was noted in the earliest systematic research on race and probation (Commission for Racial Equality, 1981) and in later studies; this has also been linked to the over-representation of black people in prison. While this outcome from sentencing in the Crown Courts may be partly explained by the larger proportion of black defendants pleading not guilty and therefore not being subject to pre-trial reports in which the option of supervision might have been explored (Moxon, 1988) this is itself an example of a probation service practice working, in combination with other elements of the system, to produce an objectively discriminatory outcome. The high incidence of not-guilty pleas may itself be a consequence of black defendants having been charged with more serious offences when less serious charges could have been brought. When taken together with report content incorporating cultural stereotypes as documented by Whitehouse (1983) and others, the need for an anti-discriminatory approach to report writing is clear, and this awareness has informed much of the in-house 'gatekeeping' or pre-hearing scrutiny of reports which has become widespread service practice in recent years.

Similarly, concern about recommendations in reports on women arose from a number of disconcerting findings: for example, that women receiving a first custodial sentence tend to have fewer previous convictions than men at the corresponding point in a penal career; that this may be partly a consequence of women being recommended for probation at too early a stage; and that they may also be missing out on access to other non-custodial options such as Community Service (see, for instance, Dominelli, 1984). A recent large-scale study of the content of the social inquiry reports (Gelsthorpe, 1991) has found continuing cause for concern: although there was little evidence of overt racist or sexist language, perhaps as a result of greater awareness of these issues in the past few years, there remained considerable evidence of a differential approach: for example, women's offending, as compared to that of men, was more often attributed to social and welfare problems or psychological difficulties; access to community service was still a problem; and reports on women laid greater stress on the domestic environment, to the extent that they were far more likely than men to receive a home visit from the reporting probation officer. Now that the 1991 Criminal Justice Act itself requires a non-discriminatory approach to criminal justice, and the Home Office national standards for pre-sentence reports emphasise its importance, there is all the more reason for probation officers to continue their scrutiny of this aspect of practice. Proposals and content need to be linked in a comprehensive approach to quality in reporting, and this should also contribute to reducing discrimination and encouraging more equal justice.

Assessing the quality of reports

To what extent is concern about the overall quality of reports still justified? Or does this simply focus critical attention on probation officers which could be better directed to other parts of the system? Until recently this would have been a difficult question to answer: as the last chapter shows, problems persisted but it was difficult to form an overall view of their prevalence or extent. However, another recent study carried out in preparation for the 1991 Act (Gelsthorpe and Raynor, 1992) enables us partly to close this gap, as it provided an opportunity to carry out a quality audit of a number of reports and also to ascertain the views of sentencers in the Crown Courts about reports in general and about the quality and usefulness of particular reports presented to them.

The study arose from the Act's requirement, described in the previous chapter, that a sentencing court must normally obtain and consider a pre-sentence report in a number of cases where a social inquiry report was previously optional, and quite often not prepared if no pre-trial report was available and a report would have required a further adjournment following a conviction or a late change of plea. This led to concern about the number of additional reports and the resources needed to produce them, and about possible delays, further adjournments and perhaps more remands in custody when a plea of not guilty prevented the preparation of a pre-trial report. In order to form a clearer view of the problems involved and of the additional resources required, the Home Office and the Lord Chancellor's Department co-operated to set up pilot studies in five Crown Courts during the summer of 1991. A particular concern was whether the probation service could produce post-trial reports at short notice in cases where it was particularly important to avoid delay, and whether reports produced at short notice would be of a satisfactory standard.

The quality of reports was a particularly sensitive issue in these studies, since there existed no generally accepted way to measure the quality of reports, and little reliable knowledge about what sentencers in the Crown Courts thought about the reports normally produced for their use. The method developed by the researchers involved two rather different and complementary approaches. One involved the systematic appraisal of a sample of 142 reports produced in the pilot courts. The other consisted of a series of interviews with sentencers in those courts about their views on reports generally, and in particular their opinions about three selected reports which had recently been presented in some of their own cases, and were also appraised by the researchers in addition to the main sample.

The quality appraisal instrument was based on existing official guidance and established probation service theory and practice regarding social inquiry reports, with particular emphasis on those aspects of social inquiry practice which seemed likely to carry over into the new world of pre-sentence reports. Important influences were Bottoms and Stelman (1988), Raynor (1980 and 1985) and Gelsthorpe (1991). The choice and weighting of items also reflected experience gained in team audit exercises and in-service training, and in the design of checklists and appraisal instruments for these. The exercise eventually involved 42 variables falling mainly under 5 headings. These concerned how well the report rated on coverage of relevant background; on balanced and objective presentation of the defendant; on coverage of the current offence and previous offending if relevant; on coverage of sentencing options; and on overall style, readability and presentation. These five subscores added together to make an overall quality score. The instrument used was a precursor of the Quality Assessment Guide for pre-sentence reports later produced by the same researchers (Gelsthorpe, Raynor and Tisi, 1992; see also the Appendix of this book, which reproduces one version of the QAG to illustrate for the reader the type of appraisal involved). The appraisals were carried out by three researchers, all of whom had substantial experience of research on social inquiry reports and, in two cases, experience of preparing them in former occupations as probation officers. Regular joint appraisal exercises were also conducted to ensure consistency of approach. Appraisals were carried out 'blind' without knowing the preparation times allowed for particular reports, and then compared with the Home Office monitoring data which included preparation times. The resulting tables covered hundreds of pages of printout, and readers interested in the detail are referred to the full report (Gelsthorpe and Raynor, 1992); however, some findings are of particular relevance for the issues discussed in this chapter.

The most important finding for immediate practical purposes was that the average quality of the short-notice reports did not differ significantly from the average quality of reports for which longer preparation times had been allowed. This was reflected in the guidance eventually given by the Home Office to the probation service and the Crown Courts about development of the pre-sentence reporting system. In fact, the quality of reports was very uneven and inconsistent regardless of the time available. The impact of earlier research and writing on consistency of practice in reports had clearly been less than is sometimes believed. The short-notice reports contained roughly the same range of poor and good reports as was found among the rest of the sample, and although the best reports were impressive, some of the poorer ones were very weak. It is clearly important that the introduction of national standards for reports should be supported by training and quality control procedures which will help to eliminate the lower end of this range. In passing, it is worth noting that the majority of reports contained errors of spelling, grammar or punctuation, usually minor but occasionally not. It was also worrying to see that most reports still devoted more space to the subject's social history than to discussion of either offending or sentencing.

Although in general the differences between reports had little to do with the time available for their preparation, there were a few differences between short-notice reports and the rest which have practical implications. Faster reports tended, on average, to be less thorough in their discussion of offending, perhaps because, with some offenders, more than one interview is needed to arrive at a clear and realistic picture of a pattern of offending. The faster reports were also less likely to have used information from any source other than the defendant, the court proceedings and probation service records. Relatives, partners, employers or other useful contacts in the community were more likely to figure in reports when more time was available. Similarly, when short-notice reports discussed the possibility of a probation order they were less likely to suggest 'packages' involving additional requirements or facilities which needed to be arranged with third parties. This could tend to exclude defendants subject to fast reports from consideration for a day centre place, for example. It was therefore recommended that when local arrangements for short-notice post-trial reports were being developed, procedures should be introduced which allow the probation service to seek a longer adjournment for more thorough investigation in a minority of cases which are initially thought suitable for a fast report but turn out to involve unexpected complexities.

The research also tried to identify any differences in the way report writers had approached different groups of offenders. It was not possible to draw any reliable conclusions about reports on black people, as these proved not to have been consistently identified in the local completion of the Home Office monitoring forms; however, some differences were found between reports on women and men. Reports on women were of slightly poorer average quality, mainly because they tended to be assessed as weaker in their coverage of offending; they were also much less likely than men to be judged suitable for community service. Women also figured prominently in reports on men, for example as partners or mothers. An argument with or temporary separation from a partner was often advanced as a kind of mitigation to explain why a man went 'off the rails', perhaps in a drinking spree which ended in a burglary or a fight. Alternatively, a new or reconciled partner would be represented as a reason why offending would not occur in future. One woman managed to appear in both roles, as provoker of past offending and insurance against future misdemeanours. This gives rise to some concern that if male offenders are encouraged to believe that their offences are caused or prevented in this way, this may not help them to take responsibility for their own offending or non-offending.

Judges' views of reports

The interviews with judges and recorders (fifteen in all, involving two judges and one recorder in each of the pilot areas) proved to be a very useful way of gaining views on the quality of reports in the study and on ideal conceptions of reports. The view which emerged was that good reports identify sources of information, are reasonably concise, dated, well set out, logical and consistent. They contain background information on defendants where this is relevant to an understanding of offences, and discuss offences beyond a mere rehearsal of facts already known to the sentencer and beyond the defendant's version of particular incidents: for example, they could cover reasons for the offence, motivation and defendants' attitudes to their offences. Good reports manage to convey to the sentencer something about the defendant 'as a person'. Whilst background information is important, sentencers do not want it to swamp reports.

They also express concern about 'unrealistic' recommendations. These were often a matter of language, and it was clear that sentencers wish to find reasoned argument, not mere assertion, as to why one sentencing option might be appropriate and not another. Sentencers did offer the view that there seemed to be fewer and fewer unrealistic recommendations presented to them, but that a report which glossed over the whole issue of proportionality would be a very weak report indeed. Some suggested that the 'unrealistic' recommendation often arises from the probation officer having limited information – from the defendant only perhaps – and failing to reflect the gravity of the offence. Although they tended not to be clear about exactly how it should be done, sentencers wanted some indication that the probation officer appreciated the issue of seriousness. However, an unusually lenient recommendation would not be dismissed out of hand if presented by an experienced and known probation officer, justified in detail and acknowledged as unusual. When community penalties might be an option, sentencers expected reports to tell them what might be done with the offender in the community, how a particular sentence would address problems and what it would mean in terms of what the offender had to do. As one sentencer put it, he wanted the probation officer to tell him why help was needed, what form it could take and how it might have some effect on the defendant. Probation officers were identified by some sentencers as the only credible source of this kind of information.

The issue of how much detail is to be included in reports is complicated by the fact that different sentencers have different degrees of knowledge about particular probation order conditions and other community options. Sentencers suggested that the experienced judge, who has participated in liaison meetings, has an established relationship with the court liaison probation officer and who has perhaps even visited the local 4B Day Centre, will require fewer details of community options than the part-time recorder or newly appointed judge. However, the general view was that reports should provide full details of proposed community sentences, if necessary in a separate appendix to the report, as if the report writer did not know who might be sentencing a particular defendant.

Interestingly, in an exercise designed to compare sentencers' assessments of a set of reports and the researchers' appraisals of the same reports, there was little difference in the respective assessment of their quality. The sentencers' assessments (on a questionnaire which used some questions drawn from the specially designed appraisal instrument and from other research instruments produced by the researchers with regard to the style, presentation, content, appropriateness of sentencing suggestions and so on) differed from the researchers' in only seven cases. In other words, the researchers agreed with sentencers' judgements of what was an 'adequate' or 'inadequate' report in 82 per cent of a total of 39 reports. The proportion in which they agreed or differed by only one point was 97 per cent of cases.

This degree of agreement about which reports are good does not, of course, mean that sentencers will always agree even with good report writers, but it does help to support the view that quality in reports is not simply a matter of individual taste. It seems that there is a basis for some consensus about the nature and purposes of a useful report: for example, it was clear that sentencers regarded the production of good reports as a skilled task, not reducible to a mechanical listing of facts. Their interest in information which helps to individualise the offender and to clarify reasons, attitudes and motivation resembles important elements in the training and professional culture of social work and helps to demonstrate the continuing importance of social work skills in probation work. A further analysis of the outcomes of the sample reports (in Gelsthorpe, Raynor and Tisi, 1992) suggested that a shared conception of what makes a good report can have substantial practical implications for sentencing: of those reports judged to be above the average quality level, 25 per cent resulted in community sentences (probation or community service) and 39 per cent in immediate custodial sentences, while the corresponding figures for 'below average' reports were 16 per cent community sentences and 48 per cent immediate custody. These differences did not reflect significant differences in the offenders or their offences, and although the numbers are fairly small, they suggest quite strongly that better reports are likely to be more successful in enabling sentencers to pass community sentences with confidence and to rely less on imprisonment.

Strategies for improving quality and consistency

The problems identified by this and other research have emphasised a need to develop effective quality control and quality assurance in pre-sentence reporting practice, and the remainder of this chapter introduces a number of ways in which probation officers and the service have attempted to do this, together with some observations from recent research about the potential of various approaches.

Broadly speaking, professional training and government guidelines have tended to reflect the state of knowledge or theory at the time, but there have (perhaps fortunately!) been no straightforward ways of ensuring that practice reflects these. Probation officers learn to write reports by a process in which imitation and socialisation into a professional culture play important parts, and a Home Office study of two decades ago (Davies and Knopf, 1973) showed how the time taken to prepare a report appeared to be determined by what was normal in the team rather than any other factor. This reminds us of two facts of central importance in any attempt to improve practice: knowledge and experience of writing social inquiry and pre-sentence reports is to be found among probation officers rather than anywhere else, and teams are important in maintaining or reinforcing both good and bad practice. These are not the products of individual vices or virtues but generated and reinforced by training and the everyday context of practice; quality is a collective responsibility.

(i)   Tariff guidance

During the 1980s approaches to improving the quality of reports were broadly of four kinds: guidance on tariff levels and targetting; 'gatekeeping'; team-based quality audits; and the more traditional practice of sample inspections by management and/or Home Office inspectors. We will concentrate on the first three, more innovative approaches. The first of these, the tariff guidance approach, was intended primarily to identify proposals appropriate to the perceived seriousness of the situation, so that intended 'alternatives to custody' should not be used by offenders who were not at risk of custody anyway, thus under-mining the credibility of programmes and risking inappropriate assignment of minor offenders to over-intensive intervention. These concerns were similar to attempts to avoid net-widening in juvenile justice, and were reinforced by findings such as that for first offenders, reconviction was twice as likely when they were on probation as when they were fined (Walker *et al.*, 1981). The most common instrument used for this purpose was the 'Risk of Custody' scale invented in Cambridgeshire (Bale, 1987), and although some officers resented its implied directiveness as a threat to their autonomy, and others may have filled the form in less accurately than was intended, most came to welcome it as a useful instrument and as a guard against capricious or arbitrary recommendations. Its widespread use, sometimes without local validation, left certain problems unresolved: was it meant to be predictive, telling you what the Court would do, or normative, telling you what it should do? Should your recommendation be designed to fit in with a predicted outcome or to influence the Court towards a different outcome? What about determinants of suitability for particular orders or programmes other than the risk of custody (ROC) score? And surely if probation services were successful in influencing courts away from custodial sentences, would this not itself tend to invalidate the scale as a predictor? Despite these and other problems, ROC scales made a very useful contribution as a monitoring instrument and a general guide as to which offenders were likely to be viewed more seriously than others. In keeping with the sentencing practice of its time, it attached great weight to previous convictions, and its post-1991 Act equivalents, the emerging 'seriousness' scales, are more in keeping with the proportionality principle.

(ii)   Gatekeeping

ROC scales have figured particularly strongly in the central monitoring of social inquiry practice by senior management and in sample inspections, which have often been used to provide a year-by-year measure of whether reports in a particular area are being targetted in accordance with local policy. Sometimes these issues of tariff-appropriateness are also raised in pre-court scrutiny of reports, with a view to changing them if necessary: this was a widespread practice in juvenile justice agencies in the late 1980s, where it came to be called 'gatekeeping'. In probation this kind of tariff monitoring is more likely to be done retrospectively, as a form of quality assurance, and the term 'gatekeeping' tends to be used for scrutiny by a senior probation officer, or more often by colleagues in the team, which focuses particularly on content and aims to identify and weed out any discriminatory language.

   This can be a controversial process, particularly if it is seen as a threat to officers' autonomy at the same time as producing allegations of racism or sexism, and in a few teams it may be difficult to question the process without inviting allegations of this kind. Certainly there seem to be problems when it is pursued by a few enthusiasts without broad team support and when it concentrates on a narrow range of issues. Gatekeeping needs to be carried out through skilled and supportive communication: many officers have found it helpful to work in pairs providing mutual consultation on reports, but team-based gatekeeping can be a mixed experience. We are aware of teams in which some officers have routinely avoided presenting reports to gatekeeping panels when particular individuals are members, and of a panel which approved a report only to reject the same report when presented again on another day when the panel members were different. However, gatekeeping does seem to have worked against the conscious or unconscious use of discriminatory language, and at least one study shows a positive effect on quality of reports when gatekeeping uses agreed criteria and procedures, addresses a range of quality issues, and operates with team and management support (Northumbria Probation Service, 1989). Interestingly the team producing the weakest reports in that study contained more experienced officers who seem to have worked in the more traditional autonomous (or isolated) manner.

(iii)   Team audit

One of the most promising strategies for directly influencing report-writing practice seems to be the team audit, quite widely used now as a form of in-service training, based either on office teams or on groups of peers brought together specifically for the event. In this kind of exercise officers look together at each other's reports, carry out a quality appraisal, discuss it, share experiences and give each other advice, often using an agreed schedule or checklist of headings for appraisal. (In fact the quality appraisal instrument used in the PSR pilot study was partly derived from a team audit training checklist, and the Quality Assessment Guide in the Appendix can also be used for this purpose.) These exercises can be carried out on a sample of reports prepared over a particular time period, or using reports on particular categories of client, or using particular types of report, for example by asking participants to bring copies of a report in which they argued unsuccessfully in support of a community sentence. The report writer should be involved in the assessment, with adequate time allowed for discussion. As is so often the case with promising practices in probation, there has been little formal evaluation of this kind of process: one exception, however, is the study reported by Campbell and Denney (1991) which shows an improvement in report writing after training. Interestingly the reported improvements included changes in the way offences were explained, with an increased emphasis on the immediate situation and context, and less on problems in the family. It should also be noted that this kind of exercise can be used specifically to appraise and target practice in relation to particular groups – for example, all reports on women or all reports on black people – and thus to reinforce the anti-discriminatory approach identified at the beginning of this chapter as essential to equal justice.

Conclusion: assuring quality

It seems possible that gatekeeping, at its best, incorporates the elements of dialogue, collaboration and learning from peers which also make this kind of training successful. Similarly, there would seem in theory to be scope for increasing consistency by basing training, gatekeeping, monitoring and inspection on similar criteria and indicators of quality, which is often not the case at present. Indeed, it is not uncommon to find a service basing its monitoring of reports on one list of indicators, while teams in the same service carry out gatekeeping based on their own different lists. During the summer of 1992, in the last few weeks before the implementation in the Criminal Justice Act, the Home Office commissioned a study of these issues in the hope that a consistent national approach to quality assurance might be developed, and one of the authors participated in it (Gelsthorpe, Raynor and Tisi, 1992).

This study incorporated a wide-ranging survey of quality control and monitoring systems being applied by probation services to social inquiry reports, or developed by them with the imminent introduction of pre-sentence reports in mind, and revealed a wide diversity of systems in use, ranging from the quite sophisticated to the patchy and idiosyncratic. There was little evidence of a common approach across probation services, except where a number of services had independently adopted similar devices, such as 'risk of custody' scales, and even these were often used in varying ways and were in any case mostly destined for replacement by 'seriousness' scales. In some areas, quite different procedures and criteria were in use even in neighbouring teams, sometimes with very little connection or consistency with criteria or processes at County level. The research team came to the conclusion that a more consistent system based on a more comprehensive range of criteria with, where possible, a clearer empirical basis would be preferable, and the Quality Assessment Guide (see Appendix for one version) was developed and tested as an approach to this. In the future it may be possible to build up a useful database of pre-sentence report quality monitoring using comparable methods and criteria, so that, for example, the impact of National Standards on practice could be assessed; however, at the time of writing this kind of work is still in its infancy and much research remains to be done.

What is clear, however, is that as a result of an empirical approach to practice, quality in reports to courts can now be, to some extent at least, identified and measured by consistent criteria that have their roots in good social work practice and in an understanding of the report's function in the criminal justice process. Such assessment methods can be used in training and monitoring, and there is some evidence that they can now be related to the perceptions of sentencers and to the effectiveness of reports. The prospects for more effective practice in influencing the criminal justice process are exciting; the next two chapters explore some similar themes in those parts of the service's work that aim to influence the offenders themselves.

5

'Some Things Do Work': The New Evidence

Introduction

The production of consistently persuasive pre-sentence reports is, as we have argued in the two previous chapters, a vital ingredient in the process of influencing the system so that probation officers are allowed the opportunity to intervene effectively, not only in people's offending patterns but also on behalf of these people's welfare. Their persuasiveness is dependent, in part, on the availability of tangible and relevant programmes and strategies aimed at effecting changes in individuals and their circumstances. It also follows that the writing of reports which communicate in an effective and an anti-discriminatory way is likely to be much easier to achieve if the report writer can present a 'belief driven' option for the court to consider. It is to this area of practice that we now turn.

Earlier we referred to the fact that practitioners had, in the face of generally pessimistic research findings about their activities, continued to want to help their clients, and to believe that they could do so. As a consequence the work of the service during the seventies and the eighties continued to have strong rehabilitative and reformative components. Despite this, the growing dominance of the diversionary objective (via the provision of alternatives to custody and what has been described as the obsession with 'input measurement') provides an indication of a lack of confidence in change-directed effort (Humphrey and Pease, 1992). The negative research findings of the seventies have been well documented, and it is not our intention to repeat them (Raynor, 1985; McGuire and Priestley, 1990; May, 1991; Vass, 1990).

Our concern in this chapter is with reasons for optimism rather than pessimism, so we will now describe some concrete examples which might inform British probation practice through the nineties and into the next century, and in doing so consider some of the evidence of successful work. There is, indeed, a plethora of emerging studies which counter the negative findings referred to above, but we do not wish to submerge the reader under their collective weight. Instead, we will outline a small number of studies and draw out the key features which should inform current and future practice.

The reasoning and rehabilitation programme

This is a Canadian example of a systematically applied piece of work which reveals some exciting potential (the detail of this programme forms the basis of work in this country which will be expanded upon in the next chapter). It is based on a number of 'sequential research studies', the first being an examination of rehabilitative programmes undertaken in North America between 1973 and 1978 (Ross *et al.*, 1988). Having discovered reductions in recidivism ranging from 30 per cent to 74 per cent, the researchers compared the successful programmes with those which had failed, and discovered that what was different about the successful programmes was that they concentrated on people's *thinking*. They then reviewed forty years of experiments and identified particular deficiencies in the thinking skills of people who persistently offend. The final part of the project involved identifying a number of cognitive training methods and exercises which had been used in successful programmes, and incorporating them into a carefully designed training package.

Subsequently five probation officers were trained to administer the eight-hour programme and the courts were persuaded to make probation orders which were then randomly allocated to three groups – regular probation, life skills and cognitive training. A nine-month follow-up revealed results which suggest that cognitive training can reduce recidivism: they were respectively a reconviction rate of 69.5 per cent for the regular probation group, 47.5 per cent for the life skills group, and 18.1 per cent for the cognitive training group. There was also a distinct difference in the subsequent imprisonment rates: 30 per cent for the regular probation group, 11 per cent for the life skills group, and zero for the cognitive training group. These results clearly offer a different perspective on the possibilities of working successfully with people who offend regularly. Nevertheless, the probation service should consider them carefully and not rush into encouraging an uncontrolled use of the 'new toy', because the follow-up period was after all limited, and the number of people involved in the experiment relatively low. Instead it should consider other available evidence, examine the arguments for a continued focus on reform and rehabilitation, and study the characteristics of this and other successful programmes.

Meta-analytical surveys

Although the Reasoning and Rehabilitation programme is significant in its own right, it stands alongside the conclusions of a number of extensive surveys of offence-focused work. Lipsey, for instance, reviewed approximately 500 projects with young offenders (Lipsey, 1990). He selected the studies according to the following criteria:

1. The project had reduction of recidivism as its principal aim.
2. The participants were 21 years old or under.
3. There were 'measured outcome variables and quantitative results which were reported and contained at least one delinquency measure'.

4. There was comparison under control conditions with other groups.

The meta-analytical approach used entailed averaging results across a range of outcome variables. The conclusions are modest, but considering the scale of the survey they demand consideration. Whilst Lipsey acknowledges that the effects reported in the studies ranged from large to small, he found 'at least modest overall treatment effects' (p. 40). Another meta-analysis of a large number of both juvenile and adult treatment programmes draws the following conclusion:

> some service programmes are working with at least some offenders under some circumstances, and we think that helpful linkage among case, service and outcome are suggested by three principles known as risk, need and responsivity. (Andrews *et al.*, 1990)

In other words they are suggesting that promising indicators of success occur when the work is based on appropriate and proven methods and is also directed at people who persistently offend, are at high risk of re-offending, and display anti-social attitudes.

Rehabilitation and the features of successful programmes

The results discussed above undoubtedly give grounds for optimism. However, to rely solely on crime reduction results as a justification for probation involvement with rehabilitation narrows the argument, and, as we will argue later in this chapter, encourages a limited correctional stance. Punishment, with its tenuous claim to effectiveness, is the preserve of the judicial system. Offence reduction activity which is not characterised by moral force-feeding is a legitimate function of the probation service (Rumgay, 1989). The implementation of justice and the response to the complex web of social and personal disadvantage underpinning much offending is the responsibility of both; it is, indeed, a moral imperative. The argument for the probation service to be involved in rehabilitative effort, a component of which is reformative, must be pursued within an ethical context. As McWilliams and Pease succinctly and forcefully argue the case for probation officers helping to rehabilitate people: 'They should do so because it would be prudent and, much more importantly, they should do so because it is morally required' (McWilliams and Pease, 1990). The effective delivery of rehabilitation is equally important and dependent on clarity about what we now know are the features of successful projects. Before exploring this point in detail, it is useful to remind ourselves of the caveat outlined by Ross and Fabiano:

> Effective programmes are not only exceptional in their results, they are also atypical in other ways such as the type of intervention techniques they employ; the types of staff who apply these techniques (their training, their personality and their motivation); the nature of the relationship between the staff and the offenders; the degree to which they attend to the social, situational and economic factors which affect their clients; and the intensity and duration of the programme. (Ros and Fabiano, 1985)

For a delineation of the features of these projects which appear to be successful in fulfilling their aims we rely heavily on the extensive survey and analysis of the literature on sanctions for persistent offenders undertaken by Gill McIvor (1990). They are as follows:

1. **An offence and problem solving focus.** This involves a concentration on helping people to resolve or learn ways of resolving these problems which are judged by worker and client to be linked to offending. It does not mean a confined probing of the offence or offences but rather a broader, collaborative and relevant problem-solving effort (Priestley *et al.*, 1978).

2. **High risk offenders.** We now know that intensive and intrusive work with people whose offending history is light

at best achieves nothing at all and probably makes matters worse by dragging people unnecessarily into the system. The evidence points clearly to the necessity (if 'net-widening' is to be avoided) of ensuring that the target group for any intensive programme consists of people who have a persistent pattern of offending and who are judged to be at high risk of further offending and custody.

3. **Multi-faceted interventions**. Reliance on one approach or method is likely to be counter productive, but this is not to suggest an unconsidered 'scatter-gun' approach. Workers need to think clearly about which particular method is likely to be successful with what particular problem per person. This requires not only having a range of reliable methods to choose from but also an approach to working with people which is based on collaboration. In this respect the Reasoning and Rehabilitation programme, which combines a range of well tried and tested methods into a properly sequenced programme, provides a useful template.

4. **Concrete services which are relevant to people's needs**. Although McIvor's survey is helpful on this point, it needs no more than the direct experiences of practitioners and the voice of offenders to lead us to the conclusion that the success of work is determined by the degree to which people's needs are addressed. If an individual has a drug dependency, little money, no job and poor accommodation, individual psychotherapy aimed at heightening awareness of distorted thinking patterns is destined for limited success! Lipton and his colleagues suggest that even therapy, if it is to be effective, needs 'a pragmatic orientation' (that is, is oriented towards 'street' problems) and not a 'psycho-analytical orientation' (Lipton *et al.*, 1975).

By reference to the work of Petersilia (1990), McIvor also usefully outlines a set of conditions necessary for the survival of programmes.

a. **Clarity of purpose**. The programmes which do survive are based on a very clear idea of their rationale; in other words, they have clear aims towards which the change effort is directed.

b. **Receptive environment**. As Raynor's work in West Glamorgan demonstrates, survival is dependent on the acceptance and support provided from within and outside the organisation (Raynor, 1988). A pertinent example from recent probation history is the Day Training Centre experiment, which can be seen to have suffered from the process of marginalisation that can occur when a specialist unit is not fully owned by the rest of the service (Vanstone and Raynor, 1981; Vanstone, 1993).

c. **Simple change**. Complex and rapid change can be stressful and undermining. Organisations setting up an intensive programme should therefore not over-complicate the changes required to implement it.

d. **Committed leadership**. Too often innovation from the grass roots withers and dies either because it is starved of resources, or because the motivated practitioner(s) move(s) on. Intensive work, therefore, needs to be fully supported, serviced and led by management believers who provide sufficient resources and clear lines of authority (Lewis, 1991; Thomas and Vanstone, 1992).

e. **Practitioner ownership**. If the programme is spawned by the creativity of the practitioner, ownership is guaranteed. On the other hand, if it is a 'top-down' initiative it is fundamentally important for it to be explained to, and negotiated with, those whose task it is to deliver it. Moreover, practitioners need to be involved at the stages of setting up, planning and preparation, and will need to feel a real sense of power and influence over the shape of the programme.

Broader measures of success

We have so far looked at some of the evidence of success in reducing recidivism and at the key features identified as consistent with that success. In doing so we began the argument against a reliance on one measure of effectiveness, namely crime reduction, on the grounds that the probation service has a moral responsibility to concern itself with issues of disadvantage and injustice, and with help to offenders. We accept McWilliams and Pease's (1990) definition of that help as 'a moral good expressed by the probation service on behalf of the community'. Concern with rehabilitation implies a broad base for probation work, and that in turn prescribes a broad definition of the term 'effectiveness'. However, broadness does not mean being unspecific and woolly. Certainly one of the positive results for the service of a concern for 'consumers' has been a recognition of the need for accountability. A genuine care for the plight of the poorest sections of our communities is surely confirmed by a commitment to clarity of action, monitoring, measurement of impact and a desire to guard against unintended consequences. The probation service, therefore, must concern itself with what the 'left realists' describe as the 'square of crime' – offender, victim, state agencies and the public (Young, 1991) – and in pursuing effectiveness must seek answers in a number of different directions. Later in this chapter we will examine in more detail some British examples of success in the area of crime reduction, but first let us look at those different directions.

Anti-poverty strategies

When clients are asked about the reasons for their offending, shortage of money appears high on the list. In their daily contact with people probation officers have to deal with the effects of poverty, and more specifically with the results of both the changes in benefit provision and the growth of unemployment since 1979. The emergence of an 'underclass' and the difficulties encountered by probation clients have been thoroughly documented (Jordan, 1990; Stewart *et al.*, 1989). Knowledge of this grim reality is one thing, dealing with it so that some of the effects of poverty are ameliorated is another. At an individual level problems often seem intractable; it is, therefore, vitally important for the service to establish and monitor strategies designed to address the issue on a wider front. The Social Issues Project established in 1988 provides some useful guidelines in this respect (Broadbent, 1989). It was set up to improve the skills and knowledge of probation staff in the field of social security and welfare benefits, and thereby positively change probation practice and policy; but it was also intended to forge links with other pertinent organisations. It produced some very practical guidelines for practitioners:

1. Knowledge: officers should keep up to date on legislative changes and the detail of provision; furthermore they should ensure that they distinguish between structural and individual problems. Training should be delivered specifically for these purposes.
2. Organisation: interested parties within the organisation should be brought together and both agencies and individuals should join national organisations such as Child Poverty Action; CHAR, the housing campaign for single people; the Low Pay Unit; and National Council for One Parent Families.
3. Information: this should be routinely recorded and shared with other interested people, perhaps through a bulletin or newsletter.
4. Clients: an advice/help list should be set up and clients empowered through information and referral to self-help groups.

A strategy of this kind could then be evaluated for effectiveness in respect of the extent of the network established, the quality of the information gathered and disseminated, and the resolution of individual problems.

Anti-oppressive practice

Despite some recent attempts at reassurance (Harris, 1992) we consider that the evidence discussed below provides ample ground for concern about oppression and discrimination within the criminal justice system. Those most commonly disadvantaged are black people and women, and it is to these that the white- and male-dominated probation service needs to turn its attention. In dealing with them separately we emphasize that they are two sides of the same coin.

We do not deny that attention is already being paid to the issue of race or that there are some laudable white initiatives in existence. However, we also believe that the probation service has only begun to take the first tentative steps along this path, and that it must not neglect the historical dimensions of racism, and treat it as a new discovery. Racism is not new: it is embedded in British colonial history (Fryer, 1984). Anti-discriminatory practice is a moral imperative and it is therefore the responsibility of white probation staff to develop anti-racist practice, and not to use the absence of black colleagues or clients as an excuse for inaction. If history itself is not enough, then the evidence of research findings offers a clear enunciation of the problems faced by black people. They are more likely to be criminalised, less likely to be given non-custodial options such as probation and community service, and more likely to end up in custody (de la Motta, 1984; Mair, 1986; Whitehouse, 1983; Willis, 1983). Such results suggest the institutionalisation of racism within the system itself, and consequently the actions of the probation service must be located at the level of structural as well as individual examples of racism.

Our emphasis here is on anti-racist practice in service provision, but it is important to emphasise that the starting point is the probation agency itself (Denney, 1992). The necessity of promulgating anti-racist perspectives in pre- and post-qualifying training (Collett *et al.*, 1990) and of recruiting black officers at all levels of the service is axiomatic. Unless the agency can tangibly demonstrate an anti-racist culture it is unlikely to succeed in having any significant impact on the discriminatory processes of the criminal justice system. Our attempts to identify the criteria for judging effectiveness have been considerably informed by the work of Bandana Ahmed, who delineates a checklist for a radical anti-racist social work approach (Ahmed,

1990). We have built concerns specific to work with offenders into some of the key features of her checklist to produce the following indicators of effectiveness:

1. the extent to which black people have equal access to community-based sentences which do not reinforce social control but assist rehabilitation. This will necessitate the monitoring of sentencing outcomes for black offenders reported on by probation officers;
2. the degree to which black people view the services offered by the probation service as relevant to their needs and problems;
3. how far social inquiry reports counter mythology and project a knowledge and understanding of black offenders. More monitoring for stereotypical racist language and content will need to be established;
4. the extent to which staff and committee training is effective in promoting anti-racist attitudes and actions. Particular emphasis will have to be placed on how much awareness and recognition there is of the effects of social work power combined with racism on black people.

In turning to the issue of gender, we are aware of the double jeopardy faced by black women, and also how their experience highlights the fact that challenging both racism and sexism within a conceptual framework which encompasses all forms of oppression is fundamental to good social work practice (Chiqwada, 1989; Dominelli, 1988). We do not pretend to originality in our discussion of women's experiences within the criminal justice system; a number of researchers and criminologists have laid the groundwork very effectively (Carlen, 1989; Mair and Brockington, 1988; Worrall, 1990). We know that women are likely to be given probation early in their criminal careers because of a welfare orientation in social inquiry reports and sentencing, but that subsequent offending leads to a harsher response. Often the response of the probation service to the needs of women is deficient to the point of compounding this process. Community-based sentences are often structured towards the needs of male offenders (Jones *et al.*, 1991). Group projects particularly often exclude women because of understandable decisions not to increase the oppression of women by placing them in male-dominated groups. Pat Carlen argues that probation officers operating within what she calls 'a women-wise penology' could look to a number of indicators of effectiveness (in addition to those described above):

1. success in resisting the pushing of women up-tariff;
2. the extent to which non-statutory provision is available;
3. the availability of appropriate community-based sentences including community service, and all-women offence-focused groups;
4. the existence or otherwise of an informed accommodation policy for women (Carlen, 1989).

Drug misuse and harm reduction

This area of work, perhaps more than any other, illustrates the problems of relying on the reduction of offending as the only measure of effectiveness. Drug misuse (we include alcohol misuse in our definition) is usually enmeshed in complex physical, emotional and social problems and underpinned by a dependent lifestyle which can only be reshaped through small incremental changes. The work of the Sefton team in Merseyside and the Demonstration Unit in Inner London stems from a recognition of the growing problem and an acceptance of the need for a more pragmatic approach (Buchanan and Wyke, 1987; Boother, 1991). Effectiveness in work with drug users might be demonstrated by increased knowledge of the effects of drugs; a reduction in HIV/AIDS risk behaviour; a lessening of the level of, or a change in, drug-taking patterns; a reduction in drug-linked crime; and the effective presentation of such achievements as success to the courts when users re-offend.

Accommodation strategies

Alongside employment, settled secure accommodation probably figures high on the list of factors contributing to crime-free lifestyles. Lack of accommodation, on the other hand, heightens the possibility of remands in custody and actual custodial sentences and, furthermore, reduces the scope for discretionary release under the auspices of the Criminal Justice Act. Knowledge about the extent of the problem in any one probation area and a strategic response to it need to be viewed as priorities ranked alongside attempts to change people's behaviour. It is one of several ways in which probation officers can make a contribution to tackling a structural problem worsened by existing housing and social security policies. The argument here is that success in collaborating in the development of accommodation projects at one end of the spectrum, and the placing of one person in accommodation at the other end, are both evidence of effective practice. Area accommodation strategies create the possibilities of such effectiveness. The work of Nick Day within a community development resource unit established by the Devon probation service provides an interesting example (Day, 1988).

Reduction of harm caused by the criminal justice system

Although there is growing evidence of successful interventions in the lives of offenders, it is important not to lose sight of the body of established knowledge about the harm caused by the system itself. We know that many juveniles if left alone 'grow out of crime'; we are aware that supervision inappropriately applied to 'light end' adult offenders can often at best achieve nothing, and at worst have a negative effect; and we daily see the evidence of the poor track record of custodial punishment in the deleterious effects that it has on the lives of persistent offenders. Probation officers' efforts need to continue to be directed towards diversionary work in these areas. The capacity of information systems to measure effectiveness in this respect is well established and, therefore, needs to be sustained.

Reduction of harm caused to victims of crime

In one sense the probation service's concern with reduction of offending reflects a parallel concern with victims. However, we have already alluded to deficient victim awareness among offenders and the growing body of knowledge about who victims are, what they experience and what needs they express (McGuire and Pointing, 1988). As we describe later in Chapter 7, there are some interesting examples of projects which focus on the new, and relatively untested, area of offender – victim mediation (Smith *et al.*, 1988; Nation and Arnott, 1991). Nevertheless, measurement of effectiveness in responding to victims' needs, through assisting victim support schemes and direct probation involvement as described in the South Yorkshire and Devon Schemes, is pertinent to any evaluation of the overall contribution of the service.

Promising initiatives in Britain

We have quite deliberately devoted significant space to illustrating how the probation service can, and should, adhere to a multi-faceted definition of effectiveness. The reduction of recidivism will remain, however, a central expectation of the service, but it can now work towards that expectation with renewed and realistic optimism and confidence. Earlier in the chapter we outlined some promising research findings, mainly from North America; interested readers can also look to the numerous examples of successful work with offenders in the field of psychology (Priestley and McGuire, 1985). Now, however, we intend to follow the trail of British probation initiatives which show equal promise, but not before pausing and noting the paucity of studies of one-to-one work within standard probation orders. That remains a gap to be filled. The projects that we will describe vary in their focus and the rigour and purity of their research design; some of the conclusions are tentative and not all the work is unique or original. They are chosen because they each demonstrate the possibilities of success in their respective areas, and they exhibit a concern to place practice within an evaluative framework. In this sense they are relatively rare.

The Somerset Alcohol Education Group

This was a three year evaluation study involving 152 clients (Singer, 1991). The methods used were similar to those employed on other alcohol education courses run within other probation services (Bailey and Purser, 1982; Doherty *et al.*, 1990). Its lineage can be traced back to the social skills and personal problem-solving model of the late seventies (Priestley *et al.*, 1978). The programme itself was prescriptive and consisted of six group sessions 'top-and-tailed' by one-to-one counselling sessions which were meant to prepare for participation in the programme, to review the learning and to formulate a subsequent work plan. The objectives of the course were to increase the participants' knowledge of alcohol; to promote responsible drinking attitudes and behaviour; and to achieve harm reduction. A majority of those attending the group were between 17 and 24 years of age and at risk of further offending and custody; Singer adds weight to this data by firstly comparing (by types of offence) the target group with probationers and prison receptions nationally, and secondly by identifying close similarities between the target group and the prison group in relation to violent offences. They attended within the legal framework of Schedule 11 4A of the Criminal Justice Act 1982.

In his description of the evaluation Singer notes the limitations of a research framework which does not involve random allocation to an experimental and a control group, but this is balanced against the fact that the framework involves a number of differently focused measures. A further point of interest in this study lies in its use of expertise within a service (via its research and information officer) to evaluate its own practice, rather than relying on a college-based researcher, and thus reducing the problem of research being remote from practice. An alcohol knowledge test, a drink profile questionnaire, a drink diary, a consumer questionnaire and reconviction data were all used. The results are interesting and encouraging.

Alcohol knowledge test: by averaging the response scores before and after, Singer discerns a 50 per cent increase in participants' knowledge of alcohol.

Drink profile questionnaire: the Likert-style schedule, which consists of 25 questions around attitudes and behaviour towards drink, produces a risk score rating. A reduction in the risk rating is seen to be a shift towards more responsible attitudes. 72 per cent of the participants exhibited a reduced score in the post-course application of the questionnaire.

Drink diary: the subjectivity of this measure and the possibility of under-recording of alcohol consumption is accepted. With this caveat, 72 per cent reported either a maintenance of the same level of intake or a reduction.

Consumer feedback: asking offenders how they view the service being offered is not an automatic ingredient of probation-related research, but usefully in this study all participants were interviewed, and only two indicated that the course had not been worthwhile.

Reconviction data: during the twelve-month follow-up 63 per cent of the sample had no recorded convictions. This finding needs to be seen within the context of a reasonably high criminal profile (an average of 7 previous convictions).

The Afan Alternative

This is a long-established community-based alternative to custody for 17 to 25 year-olds, who again are seen to be in the high-risk category as far as re-offending is concerned. The project was evaluated between 1980 and 1987 by one of the present authors (Raynor, 1988). The groupwork approach, which involves psychodrama, sociodrama, offence-centred exercises and problem-solving methods, is certainly unique in Wales and possibly in Britain. Although there was no random allocation to experimental and control groups, Raynor compared the participants in the group and the prison population across a number of variables, namely previous convictions, principal offence type and experience of previous custody. In this way he was able to establish a close similarity in the criminal profiles of the two groups.

Two basic measures were used, firstly, recorded reconvictions at various points over a two-year follow-up period, and secondly, a self-report problem checklist. The checklist, which is an adaptation of the Mooney Problem Checklist, applies a three-point scale (serious problem, a problem, no problem) to a range of practical and inter-personal problems. It was administered to each participant by the researcher at the beginning and end of the programme.

The findings indicate a decrease in the level of reported problems. It is not certain that this was the direct result of the programme, and all that is claimed is that the offenders saw themselves as having fewer problems at the end of the programme than they did at the beginning. It is the correlation of the problem levels with the reconviction study which is much more interesting. The study found a significant reduction in the re-offending rates of the experimental group, with the best results achieved by the older, more highly convicted people. Not far behind these were younger offenders with less serious criminal profiles and few problems. The worst results were with the young offenders who had a less serious criminal profile but many problems. The importance of this finding lies not just in the significant reduction in offending but the interesting possibilities that it raises about the matching of particular levels of supervision with particular typologies of criminal and problem profile. It is, therefore, a confirmation of the risk principle referred to above.

Hereford and Worcester Young Offender project

This is a study of a Schedule 11 day centre (Roberts, 1989). Its programme is structured around a three-day week over a seven-week period; a fourth day involves the participants in reporting to their probation officer and linking with some community-based activity. Additionally the participants spend one week at an adventure training centre. The methods used include offending behaviour exercises, social skills, drama, role play and motor mechanics. Indeed, the programme closely resembles the model pioneered by the original Day Training Centres.

The target group for this project are unemployed young offenders who are at risk of custody. In his evaluation Roberts compared this group with a group which matched the criminal profile because they were recommended for the programme but were sentenced to custody instead. Reconvictions were studied over a two-year follow-up period.

It was found initially that the experimental group re-convicted faster than the custody group. However when the custody group had been at liberty for a period of eight months they began re-offending at a higher rate – they rapidly caught up and overtook the day centre group. In the experimental group the greatest success was achieved with those who had the most previous convictions, were convicted of burglary and had experienced previous custody. Comparison revealed that in the category of six-plus previous convictions the reconviction rate during the two-year follow-up period for the experimental group was 71 per cent, but for the custody group it was 100 per cent.

This research is important for three reasons. Firstly, it demonstrates the potential of the use of methods well within the skill range of probation officers with persistent offenders during their most active phase. Secondly, it underscores the negative and counter-productive aspects of custodial punishment. Thirdly, it exposes the missed opportunity during the seventies and eighties of a proper and full evaluation of the Day Training Centre experiment.

We conclude this chapter with a brief account of three other projects which, although they may not match fully the evaluative structure of those already discussed, are important examples of initiatives in the kind of research-based practice in which we argue the service has to engage.

Berkeley Sex Offenders Group

This constituted a voluntary open-ended group for non-violent sex offenders run by two officers fortnightly for up to ten men (Weaver and Fox, 1984). The organisation of the group included a properly constituted selection and referral system, stated written objectives (this began in 1977), a programme rationale, consultancy from a consultant psychiatrist and a built-in evaluation over a seven-year period.

The evaluation consisted of a reconviction study and a postal questionnaire to participants, designed by a psychologist to explore the expectations of the group held by its members; the value of the group sessions themselves; the extent to which control mechanisms were learned; and other aspects of social development. The check on reconvictions was made in 1983 on 38 full members of the group, so that the actual period of follow-up varies for each member; it revealed that 30 of the men had not re-offended sexually. The questionnaire itself achieved only a 36 per cent return rate, a fact which underlines the difficulties with postal questionnaires; unaccompanied as it was by any other measures of change in attitude and behaviour, the results do not reach any level of significance. However, they did provide the group leaders with valuable feedback from some participants, which they were able to use in refining the programme.

Black Offenders' Initiative

This is a project set up by the North Thames Resource Unit and, at the time of writing, operating as a pilot to be evaluated (Jenkins and Lawrence, 1992). It emanated from research into the needs and experiences of black probation clients undertaken by Geoffrey Pearson and Duncan Lawrence of Goldsmiths' College. One of the clear findings was the need for experimentation with black-only provision.

Black probation staff helped the unit to develop the programme and approximately thirty were trained to run it. The aims of the eight-week programme, which is structured by a groupwork pack, include giving black clients the opportunity to explore their experience, helping them examine their offending, and empowerment.

At the time of writing three groups have been completed and early feedback from both group members and leaders is positive. The evaluation is meant to contribute to the further refinement of the material and the groupwork pack so that it is usable by all staff. Although it is only possible to present a partial picture of this project we think that it is worthy of mention because it is not only an example of work involving an evaluative structure and agency–college co-operation, but also one of the probation service responding in a considered way to the needs of a disadvantaged group.

West Midlands Offending Behaviour Groups

The researchers evaluated offending behaviour groups which had been run in the Sandwell division between 1983 and 1990, and the Birmingham North division during 1990 (Davies and Lister, 1992). The programmes, which focused particularly on the decision-making process leading to offences, covered, amongst other specific issues: offending behaviour analysis; alcohol and crime; reparation and the victim; police and magistrates' perspectives; and alternatives to offending. Their basic format and content were heavily influenced by Priestley and McGuire's Offending Behaviour Model (1985).

Analysis included the re-offending during the remainder of the probation order of 54 group participants, interviews with 46 group participants, and a more detailed analysis of the offending patterns of a sub-sample of 13 group participants before and after completion of the group. The researchers, whilst acknowledging some of the methodological difficulties of the evaluative exercise, maintain that they 'can offer a reasonable indication of the credibility of the offending behaviour approach as a mean of reducing offending rates' (Davies and Lister, 1992, p. 2). They support this claim with a number of findings, which include a 54 per cent reconviction rate during the remainder of the order; a slower reconviction rate than a comparison group released from custody; and a majority of group participants (54 per cent) reporting positively on the group experience.

Conclusion

We have been concerned in this chapter with presenting the growing body of evidence of successful work with offenders, whilst at the same time illustrating the variety of ways in which the probation service can demonstrate effectiveness across a range of work which is offence-related. In doing so we have emphasised the importance of giving attention not only to what we do, but to how we do it. This involves working as far as possible within clear structures and paying attention to the detail of a range of matters such as offenders' needs, appropriate methods, required resources, the integrity of programmes and the means of measuring effects. A proper commitment to evaluation provides a route to the kind of structure required, and this applies not only to projects and group programmes but also to the sometimes messy, responsive work with individual offenders. In the next chapter, we will describe in more detail an attempt by one service to set up and evaluate a training programme for persistent offenders which is based on that commitment.

6

Developing and Evaluating a Programme to Reduce Offending

Introduction

When the right programmes are offered in the right way to the right people, some things can work. This is the accumulating message of the most recent research, including the examples discussed in the last chapter. Putting these lessons into practice is, however, no simple matter: in some ways the possibility of effectiveness now poses an even greater challenge to professional thinking and skills, because the attempt to get it right may question previous practices and assumptions. We have described in the previous chapter how the professional culture of the probation service successfully maintained a degree of optimism through the 'nothing works' era, partly sustained by unfamiliarity with the research or by an expectation that research is generally unhelpful. This often co-existed with and reinforced a very individual approach to practice in which it was assumed that only the individual practitioner was entitled to take decisions about his or her work. In what we hope will be a new era of aspiration to achievable effectiveness, some cultural and attitudinal changes are likely to be needed and are, we would suggest, already occurring. Practice is already moving beyond reliance on intuition and good intentions: the service needs to be able to embrace a new approach to empirical evidence, in which research informs and guides practice decisions, and a new openness about practice which allows new learning and experience to be used. This chapter aims to illustrate some of the problems and rewards of this kind of approach by examining one of the more substantial recent attempts to enhance probation effectiveness. This project, in which two of the authors are involved, is under way in Mid-Glamorgan in Wales at the time of writing. It seeks to introduce and evaluate, across a whole medium-sized county, a structured programme of supervision to reduce re-offending among persistent and/or serious offenders. It is known as STOP (Straight Thinking on Probation), and a brief account of its development and results to date exemplifies some of the costs and benefits of an empirical approach.

STOP: Reasoning and Rehabilitation in Mid-Glamorgan

The programme is based closely on the 'Reasoning and Re-habilitation' approach developed by Robert Ross and his colleagues in Canada (Ross and Fabiano, 1985) and outlined in the previous chapter. It uses the manual produced by Ross and others at Ottawa University (Ross, Fabiano and Ross, 1989) with a few adaptations to make some of the exercises and materials more culturally appropriate to a South Wales setting. For example, assumptions about 'normal' lifestyles reflect local conditions such as the low level of car ownership among Mid-Glamorgan probationers; or at a more basic level, the original manual is mainly male-oriented, and a modified version has been prepared for work in women's groups.

Such programmes are now quite widely used; we are aware of community-based, prison-based and half-way house versions in Canada, where a thorough evaluation is being carried out by the Canadian Correctional Service (see, for example, Fabiano *et al.*, 1990). Programmes have also been developed in at least seven

US states, in Spain and in Venezuela. The Mid-Glamorgan STOP experiment was the first to be established in Britain and the first to begin to yield evaluative data about the results of the programme in a British probation context. The empirical basis of the approach, as outlined in the previous chapter, is in research on persistent offenders which showed that many of them share a pattern of ineffective thinking and unsuccessful problem-solving in interpersonal and social situations, and that programmes which show some success in reducing offending tend to contain elements which aim to affect offenders' thinking. This is not, of course, the same as arguing that crime is 'caused by' defects in thinking skills or 'cognitive deficits'; this would be particularly incongruous in Mid-Glamorgan, one of the poorest areas in Britain with some of the worst housing, highest local unemployment and highest rates of chronic illness and disability, with many offenders themselves making a connection between their offending and the restricted opportunities offered by an impoverished social environment. The point is rather that improved social and thinking skills can give people more options about how to cope with difficulties. Logically such an approach can be complementary to approaches based on improved social policy, rather than contradicting them; it could also be argued that it offers opportunities of constructive action in the interests of disadvantaged individuals even when positive social policy change is low on the political agenda.

The programme consists of 35 two-hour sessions held usually twice per week over a 17-week period, with individual 'back-up' sessions for those who unavoidably miss a group session. The sessions are run normally by pairs of field-team probation officers who have received specific training, and in order to resource the significant extra workload, the Probation Committee agreed to an extra probation officer appointment in each of the six field teams involved. The specific aims and content of the programme are outlined by the Mid-Glamorgan service as being based on teaching the following skills (see Lucas, Raynor and Vanstone, 1992):

Self-control
We teach offenders to stop and think before they act: to consider all the consequences before making decisions; to formulate plans; to use thinking techniques to control their emotions and their behaviour.

Thinking skills
We teach offenders to critically assess their own thinking – to realise that how they think determines what they think and how they feel and how they behave. We teach them thinking strategies as a means of regulating their own behaviour.

Social skills
Many offenders act anti-socially because they lack the skills to behave in any other way. We teach a large number of skills which will help them achieve acceptance rather than rejection in social situations (eg. responding to criticism; apologising; negotiating instead of demanding ...).

Values enhancement
We use a number of group discussion techniques and a large number of commercially available games to teach values; specifically, to move the offenders from thinking only of themselves to a position of thinking about the needs of others.

Victim awareness
In our programme, we teach the offender to consider the feelings of other people and to understand the effects of their behaviour on other people – particularly their victims. While offenders remain self-centred they are bound to lack concern for their victims.

Creative thinking
To combat their fixed ways of thinking we use a number of techniques to teach offenders alternative thinking; how to consider acceptable rather than anti-social ways of responding to the problems they experience.

Critical reasoning
We teach offenders how to think logically, objectively and rationally without distorting the facts or putting the blame on others.

Social perspective taking

Throughout the programmes with all of our techniques we emphasise teaching offenders to consider other people's views and feelings and thoughts. In effect, we emphasise the development of empathy.

Their effect on others

We teach offenders how to analyse problems between themselves and others, how to understand and consider other people's values, behaviour and feelings; how to recognise how their behaviour affects other people and why others respond to them as they do.

Emotional management

An offender's success in social adjustment depends on the ability to avoid being over-emotional. We have adapted anger management techniques used by psychologists so they can be used by probation officers and can be used with other emotions such as excitement, depression, fear, anxiety ...

Helper therapy

We attempt to set up situations where the offender becomes the helper rather than being helped. It is noted that many individuals who are placed in such roles come to see themselves in a very different light and begin to attribute to themselves positive, acceptable characteristics which they would not have seen in themselves. Many examples of such changes can be observed in our Community Service projects.

It will be evident from this brief account that such a programme differs from traditional probation work in a number of ways: indeed a major focus of the evaluation of the programme has involved assessing staff reactions to this. For example, it is prescriptive; practitioners are expected to follow the manual. It is systematic, being designed to tackle particular learning tasks in a particular order, using both repetition to consolidate learning and a sequential 'building block' approach so that target skills build on and develop those already covered. Earlier attempts at social skills training in the probation service have been criticised by researchers (for example, Hudson, 1988)

for failing to apply social learning theory principles in a suffi-
ciently systematic way, and the Reasoning and Rehabilitation
approach has been developed by psychologists to avoid this kind
of problem. Perhaps the widest departures from normal practice
are in the fact that group sessions do not focus either on the
offences or on the personal problems of individual group
members: instead the targets are the specific approaches to
understanding and decision-making which are likely to be associated with offending. Individual personal difficulties and
needs for help are not of course ignored, but are dealt with
outside the group sessions as part of the normal process of
probation. The overall approach is not based on counselling,
therapy or 'treatment', but on an educational or teaching model
which aims to help probationers to learn particular useful skills.

This is perhaps best illustrated by way of some examples of
the approach. One of the major aims of the programme is to
modify the impulsive and stereotyped thinking which leads
people to repeat the same unsuccessful strategies in problematic
situations – a feature of most people's behaviour to some extent,
but one which makes a major contribution to some persistent
offenders' repeated trouble with the law. This kind of problem is
addressed in a sequential way in several parts of the programme
(for example, much of the 'Creative Thinking Skills' module),
following a first substantial introduction in the early problem
solving modules as a 'target skill: Stop and Think of all the
alternative solutions'. The aim of this session is to teach the
group members to slow down and consider alternative solutions,
and the emphasis throughout is on encouraging creativity and the
generation of alternative responses to problems.

The session starts with a cartoon on the theme 'haste makes
waste', to make the point that jumping to conclusions often leads
to errors, and the group is asked for examples of situations when
they rushed at a problem and only made it worse; their examples
are discussed in terms of the problem-solving steps they missed
out. This leads on to a series of exercises in which group
members are shown a drawing and then a number of similar
drawings, and asked to identify which is most like the original

drawing. Those who slow down and take care will (usually!) do better, and discussion is structured to draw out the strategies they are using, for example slowing down; studying details; not jumping to conclusions, etc. A number of other exercises and scenarios are used to elicit problem-solving strategies based on taking the time to consider alternatives, including some of the examples of problem situations offered by group members at the beginning. The exercises lead on to a group 'brainstorm' (with flipchart) of 'things to do' and 'things to say' in response to various problems; the application of a similar approach to a problem offered by a group member; a summary of what has been covered, and a quick evaluation by the group. The next session, on 'Consequential Thinking', introduces the next problem-solving step of choosing between alternatives by deciding which is likely to produce the best results. This sequential structure is maintained throughout the programme, with strong reinforcement of appropriate participation by group members and many opportunities for them to experience positive roles by helping in each other's learning. The core of the approach is the cumulative series of target skills, with selected learning methods appropriate to each, and implementation of the programme requires access to an authorised manual and appropriate training.

Guidance on the matching of appropriate offenders to the programme was provided for SIR writers, based on the 'risk principle' (Andrews *et al.*, 1990; McIvor, 1990) that intensive programmes are more successful if reserved for high-risk individuals and that they may be actively disadvantageous for less serious offenders.

Over 45 probation officers were sent on five-day training courses to operate the programme, constituting the majority of the main-grade workforce in the county. This reflected an intention to make the programme and the associated skills part of the standard resource of every field team, rather than confining it to a specialist group who might be perceived as exclusive or elitist. In the event, despite some initial scepticism, the training was over-subscribed and for the most part enthusiastically received. This was confirmed in a detailed evaluation by the trainers themselves (McGuire, 1991), which also involved use of the 'Theoretical Preferences Questionnaire' (developed by Nelson-Jones, 1983) to try to identify the main theoretical models which were informing officers' practice. Among the 53 officers involved in this part of the study, a 'client-centred or Rogerian' approach was most prevalent, closely followed by a 'rational–emotive' approach. Less favoured orientations were the behavioural approach and, rather to the trainers' surprise, the psychodynamic approach, which was the least popular. They comment that in view of the similarity of the rational–emotive approach to the Reasoning and Rehabilitation model, 'the results suggest that the strand of thinking that the Reasoning and Rehabilitation model encapsulates is already present among this sample of Mid-Glamorgan staff'.

Introducing and evaluating the programme

This programme represented a very substantial commitment of resources. It also formed part of a wider concern to promote and enhance the overall quality of service provision in the county. As a result, a considerable amount of work was put into informing and involving staff: a 2-day conference for all staff was followed by visits to all teams by the Chief Probation Officer and other senior managers to discuss the project and its resource requirements. Four cross-grade working parties (on research, programme construction and training, targeting and marketing) were set up and co-ordinated by a commissioning group. Further staff conferences and attendance by groups of staff at many other conferences and training courses reinforced involvement; a half-time senior appointment was allocated to assist development and research; and a substantial programme of evaluation research was built in from the start, to operate particularly during the first (experimental) year and follow up the subsequent behaviour of the first year's clients.

Evaluating a programme of this kind was of particular interest because the Home Office had tended (for instance in the 1988

Green Paper) to advocate intensive forms of supervision where the increase in intensity is primarily an increase in supervision and control and the main purpose is to allow offenders to be dealt with outside the prisons. The emphasis of this policy has been on reduction of custodial punishment rather than on influencing offenders away from crime. Many probation service interests, on the other hand, tended to emphasise their traditional commitment to professional skills in working with offenders, and would see intensive programmes, where required, as intensive help or influence rather than intensive control. Evaluating the effectiveness of the STOP programme would therefore help to throw light on how far an intensive programme based on the systematic development and deployment of probation officers' professional skills can reduce levels of subsequent offending below what would be expected following other sentences. The evaluation is also intended to assess the impact of STOP on service provision and the development of services.

While final results of the evaluation have to await the end of the planned follow-up period, one important feature of the research is regular feedback to practitioners and managers, and this has involved the production of interim reports (Raynor and Vanstone, 1992a, b; Lucas, Raynor and Vanstone, 1992). This means that some useful data have already become available. The final part of this chapter summarises some of the main findings from the evaluation exercise up to the time of writing; those requiring the full details should refer to the report of the first full year of the study (Lucas, Raynor and Vanstone, 1992), and some further output may well have become available by the time this appears in print. We hope that the full reports will be widely disseminated and used – especially among practitioners, who are still often the last to know of the findings of research.

The results of the first year

The main components of the evaluation as undertaken or started so far are:

1. An offender profile study, to identify the characteristics of STOP group members.
2. Monitoring of attendance, completions and breaches, to find out whether the demands made by a programme of this kind in the community are realistic.
3. A study of attitudes to offending and whether they change under various forms of supervision, including STOP, using before-and-after administration of the CRIME-PICS questionnaire (Frude *et al.*, 1990).
4. A study of programme integrity to determine how far the programme is being implemented in accordance with the requirements of the model. This involves systematic video observation of 55 randomly selected sessions representing 14 per cent of all sessions in the experimental year.
5. A reconviction study comparing STOP group members with various relevant comparison groups.
6. A 'consumer' study of STOP group members' views about the programme.
7. A study of probation staff reactions to the introduction and implementation of the programme.

By the end of the first year of the study, only limited progress had been made on the reconviction study, since this requires a longer follow-up period, and the attitude-change study was also incomplete in respect of probation orders without requirements, since most of these clients had not completed their orders, so that end-of-order questionnaires were not yet available to compare with those completed at the beginning. However, some limited information under both headings was available, including a comparison of recorded reconviction within six months of sentence for the STOP group and comparable offenders on 'normal' probation orders (that is, orders without requirements). Similarly, a number of CRIME-PICS results were available on a before-and-after basis for STOP clients and those on Community Service Orders, since both Community Service and the required STOP group sessions are usually completed more quickly than the normal probation order. Quite substantial information was available on other aspects of the evaluation, allowing a number of reasonably firm conclusions to be drawn.

First, it was clear from the study of offender profiles that the STOP groups were recruiting their members within the appropriate range of severity and risk. This had originally been defined as requiring a 'risk of custody' score of 55 or more, and a high assessed risk of further offending. 83 per cent of the 133 group members during the first year satisfied these criteria. The typical STOP group member was male, in his early twenties, with a 'risk of custody' score of around 75; nine previous convictions; and two previous custodial sentences. 76 per cent of the STOP group members had custodial experience. On all these measures they actually exceeded the comparison groups, that is those sentenced to 'normal' probation at a 'risk of custody' of 55 or more, those sentenced to Community Service (which required a risk threshold of 55 in Mid-Glamorgan), and those in receipt of sentences to Young Offender Institutions, suspended sentences, and sentences of 12 months or less in adult prisons. The average gravity of principal offences at the time of order or sentence was broadly comparable across these groups.

Together with the information that 80 per cent of those who were recommended for STOP but received other sentences were dealt with by immediate custodial sentences, these profiles indicated effective targeting on a group of persistent offenders at significant risk of imprisonment, very much in line with the intended target group of a cognitively-based programme designed for those who repeatedly resort to offending as a faulty problem-solving strategy or for lack of perceived alternatives.

If we exclude those group members (about 15 per cent) who did not complete the programme for legitimate reasons such as illness or finding employment, three-quarters (75 per cent) of those who could have completed the required group sessions successfully did so. Breaches for non-compliance led to about half the non-completions: the others were due to further offences, or to further offence and breach combined. A breach rate of 13 per cent compares favourably with current figures of around 18 per cent for Community Service nationally (*Home Office*

Statistical Bulletin, 13/92). This gives quite an encouraging picture of the capacity of probationers to motivate themselves and sustain commitment to a fairly demanding programme, and of the officers' success in supporting them through it.

The findings on programme integrity were similarly encouraging: only 7 per cent of the observed sessions departed from the intended design to such an extent as to pose a clear threat to the learning goals of the session. Over 70 per cent of sessions were assessed as generally positive in atmosphere, and only 9 per cent as negative. It is clearly feasible for probation officers, given appropriate materials, training, support and monitoring, to adapt their practice to accommodate the delivery of a planned programme even when, as in this experiment, a large number of officers are involved.

The preliminary results on attitude change and reconviction were necessarily based on relatively few offenders at the one-year stage, since only those who had been at risk of reconviction for at least six months could be counted. Consequently the figures were too low for any differences to be statistically significant, and these questions await fuller analysis at a later stage, when a longer follow-up period covering a full year's group members will be available. Nevertheless, some trends were indicated which will prove very interesting if continued in later figures: 35 per cent of eligible STOP group members were recorded as collecting another conviction (not necessarily serious) within six months of starting the programme, as against 42 per cent of comparable offenders subject to 'normal' probation. The available comparison on attitude change consisted of STOP and Community Service, and here it was found that increased 'crime index' scores, indicating a decrease in crime-prone attitudes and beliefs, were found in 54 per cent of Community Service clients who had by that time completed two questionnaires, and in 69 per cent of STOP group members. It would be wrong to infer too much from preliminary figures based on only a small part of a study which will eventually cover many hundreds of offenders, but these early results are certainly encouraging.

Perhaps the most interesting results so far, however, come from the people actually involved in delivering and receiving the programme. Detailed interviews were conducted by the researchers with 45 probation officers (the majority of the service) and with the first 64 offenders to complete the programme. It is not appropriate or feasible to give here a full account of all that emerged from these interviews (interested readers are referred to Lucas, Raynor and Vanstone, 1992) but they provided some of the most revealing and encouraging data generated by the study so far. For example, probation staff, often identified in other studies as disturbed by or resistant to change (May, 1991; Humphrey and Pease, 1992), showed a good grasp of the programme and its purposes; were generally positive about it when they had been involved in delivering it, as most of them had; and were likely to have used materials and methods derived from the programme in their wider work. The majority of those directly involved reported a positive change in their beliefs about the potential effectiveness of probation and the usually hidden potential of probation clients, and an increased interest in issues such as effectiveness and evaluation. Perhaps most surprising at a time when the probation service was faced with unprecedented changes and some stress due to imminent implementation of the Criminal Justice Act, a majority reported that their job satisfaction had increased and that STOP had contributed to this, despite some concerns about the resource implications of the programme and its effect on other work. Overall the staff survey gave encouraging support to the initial aim that STOP should contribute to an awareness of quality and effectiveness as achievable goals, and suggested that the decision to train and involve as many staff as possible had begun to realise some of the original hopes of a positive impact on the working culture of the organisation. It was impossible to be involved, even as an external researcher, without being impressed by the skill, creativity and commitment which the officers contributed to the programme.

The last word should belong to the group members themselves. These interviews revealed a wealth of information about the problems they faced and the reasons why they believed they offended, and about which aspects of the programme they found helpful. A few were decidedly dismissive of standard probation ('in the past it's been 'Hello, how are you?' and then the next appointment') and many found the requirement to attend irksome ('getting up early and getting here'), but most distinguished clearly between the required attendance, which seemed to be seen as the punishment component of the programme, and its aims and content, which were clearly understood by most members and regarded by 89 per cent of them as helpful – 'it looks into things deeper, made you think more instead of acting on impulse. It was a lot harder than other groups... It makes you stop and think more before you act. ...It's to help you solve your problems caused by going about it in the wrong way.' Dozens of respondents made similar points (though a few were distinctly unimpressed). Most striking, perhaps, were the explanations they volunteered of how their thinking and approach to problems had changed. 91 per cent believed there had been a positive change in their thinking, and while this by itself might not seem particularly strong evidence, it became far more convincing when supported by their own accounts of what they meant. A few examples are:

> I look into my problem. Try to work my way around it slowly. If you lose your temper you get nowhere. The other day I missed signing at the police station and I thought to myself that it was better to go in. Two years ago I wouldn't have done that.

> I sit down and work things out, whereas before I'd just drink and steal things to drink. I sit down and look at my options and work it out that way instead of rushing off and doing something stupid.

> I think about the problem, the best solution and the consequences and make sure I make the right decision ... the consequences of getting into trouble. I think more of victims now.

One respondent had thoroughly absorbed the lesson about not jumping to conclusions and (with an unconscious echo of Mao Tse-Tung's reply when asked if the French Revolution had been a success) told the researcher:

It's too early to say ... I've been out eleven months and that's the longest. I've been in prison four times so it must be doing something. I couldn't think and say that this is doing it.

Conclusion

An earlier evaluation of a programme for serious offenders in the community (Raynor, 1988) suggested that there were advantages in using methods 'with which clients can identify without too much loss of status; which make clear demands for participation; and which engage clients both cognitively and emotionally in activities relevant to problems which they actually believe they have'. Other suggested elements of effectiveness were clear objectives, explicit negotiation with potential group members, an emphasis on clients' responsibilities in the programme, clear targeting, high levels of contact and a commitment to evaluation. Experience of the STOP programme so far tends to confirm these suggestions, and reminds us also of the importance of programme integrity and specific programme content designed to bring about specific changes. Overall, the initial message is encouraging and hopeful, and shows the impact of management decisions to involve staff and engage the whole organisation in a process of positive development. Effective programmes run best in effective organisations, and we turn in the next two chapters to the theme of organising to promote change. Some things do work: how can we make more things work more often?

7

Community Responses to Crime: What Role for Probation?

Introduction

It is often suggested that the kind of focused, intensive work described in the two previous chapters entails a neglect of the wider social context of crime. The argument is that to concentrate on labelled offenders' cognitive processes and their behaviour deflects attention from issues of social and economic inequality, discrimination and oppression, and runs the risk of 'pathologising' offenders, seeing their offences as the product of individual inadequacy or wickedness, rather than as associated with problems of structural deprivation and disadvantage. If the probation service were indeed to disregard such issues, the criticism would be justified; but the rationale for this chapter is that practice with identified offenders needs to be complemented by a commitment to a broader engagement with the social problems associated with crime and criminal behaviour, and with the community's response to them. One way of expressing this is to say that the probation service should be concerned not only with questions of criminal justice, but with social justice too.

This is easy to say, but not so easy to translate into a practical, feasible programme of action (though for an early account of 'detached' probation work, see Hugman, 1977). From personal experience, we know that there has been talk in the probation service since the early 1970s (and more talk than action) of 'moving into the community', 'community involvement', 'community probation' and so on. Then and now, this interest reflects the awareness of probation officers that a purely individualised response to crime is likely to be inadequate. Recent research has provided a graphic account of the difficulties and stresses many offenders experience as a result of poverty, and how these are often exacerbated rather than reduced by the response of the social security system (Stewart *et al.*, 1989). Many of the people with whom probation officers work live in chronically straitened circumstances which offer few incentives to law-abiding behaviour. Yet, in conventional practice, officers are expected to persuade offenders that it is they who must change, and not their social circumstances, even when these circumstances may appear to make crime a rationally self-interested option (Jordan and Jones, 1988). Changes in the labour market, the widening of the gap between rich and poor, and reduced levels of social security have led these writers and others to argue that the 1980s saw the creation in Britain of an 'underclass', excluded from the 'property-owning democracy', and with few reasons to choose conformity rather than deviance. If there is such an 'underclass', there is no doubt that many of the offenders with whom probation officers work are members of it. If individual work was not enough in the early 1970s, it is certainly not enough in the early 1990s.

Faced with this weight of apparently intractable social problems, it is easy for probation officers to conclude that there is little they can do except try to alleviate immediate problems on a case-by-case basis – providing financial support, negotiating with social security officials, helping with applications to the Social Fund, and so on. This work is of course valuable and often essential if the more focused, structured work of concentrating on offending behaviour is ever to get started, or ever to be effective. But of itself it is likely to leave probation officers only too aware that they are leaving the underlying causes of crime problems in their locality untouched. The task remains of finding ways of going beyond the traditional, individualised approach of probation and making a contribution to the wider community's response to crime.

In this chapter we will first discuss what is actually meant by community involvement, and what justifies it as a relevant and appropriate aspect of probation practice. We will argue that the aims of work in the wider community have been clarified in recent years, and that crime prevention has emerged as its principal justification. We then discuss some developments in theory and policy on crime prevention which, we think, are encouraging in that they open out a space for a probation contribution. Turning to issues of practice, we note some continuing difficulties for probation officers seeking to make sense of a community orientation, and suggest how some of these might be resolved by adopting a realistic view of inter-agency co-operation. The chapter concludes with some discussion of the possible contribution of the probation service to work with victims and with a discussion of the emerging pattern of community-based strategies on crime problems.

The meaning of 'community involvement'

What is it that probation officers actually do when they attempt to become more closely involved in the community? And why do they think they are doing it? The most systematic answers to these questions are still those given by Henderson (1987). He identified three models of practice: 'community outreach', in which staff use community resources in order to help clients; 'service development', entailing inter-agency work with voluntary and statutory agencies; and 'neighbourhood work', meaning direct work with local people with the aim of helping them to set up and maintain community groups. Henderson identified five justifications, offered by services themselves, for a community-based approach. The first was crime prevention, and Henderson observed (prophetically, in view of the developments discussed below) that 'there are some voices in the Probation Service seeking to link, if not equate, prevention and community probation work. There are others, however, who have doubts as to the advisability of using that argument' (Henderson, 1987, p. 11). The enthusiasts felt that crime prevention was the obvious goal for probation involvement in the community, while the doubters were sceptical about whether they could deliver the implied promise of crime prevention, or felt that community involvement had other justifications which a crime prevention emphasis would devalue.

These other justifications were of different kinds, and less easy to define clearly. One, described by Henderson as 'crime and community', is similar to the first in being an aim, rather than a method. The argument is that in deprived neighbourhoods probation officers constantly come across problems of unemployment, housing, poverty and discrimination which impinge directly on both offenders and victims. In such communities, probation officers can act as educators and mediators, and influence local policies on crime-related problems such as alcoholism and homelessness; and they cannot ignore the community dimensions of crime and fear. Henderson distinguishes this position from the crime prevention argument by suggesting that it makes explicit the correlation between crime and other issues, takes account of fear of crime, and addresses the question of scapegoating of offenders. He also notes a concern with those on the receiving end of discrimination and with women, who are expected to carry the burden of care in these battered communities. In view of the developments in thinking about crime prevention described later in this chapter, however, it may no longer be necessary to make a distinction between this and the first justification, since the view of crime and its prevention implied in this argument is close to that which now dominates policy and practice, not least in its recognition of the needs and problems of victims.

A third justification identified by Henderson was that the probation service is or should become a 'community agency'. By this officers meant both the need to maintain links with other organisations and the issue of communicating more effectively with the public, which would increase the credibility of the service and support for its work. In addition to this public relations interest, it was felt that the notion of a 'community agency' would encourage officers to see offenders themselves in context, as members of the community. The emphasis in this position on inter-agency links was to become increasingly prominent in statements on probation and criminal justice policy in the years following Henderson's research, although it would be unduly limiting to treat 'community involvement' as synonymous with inter-agency co-operation. Finally, Henderson noted that community involvement could be seen as an element of good practice, in that knowledge of local resources would enable officers to provide a better service, and address factors underlying their clients' offending; and it was sometimes argued that the justification for a community orientation could be found in theories informing probation practice, such as the importance of networks in supporting offenders in the community.

The principal aim of wider work in the community to emerge from Henderson's analysis is, then, crime prevention, with a specific concern in the 'crime and community' strand of thinking with reconciling offenders with their communities, and thus at least an implicit interest in work with victims. As practice and policy have developed since the mid-1980s, the two themes – crime prevention and victims – have been more clearly and consistently identified as the main justifications for probation work in the community, and it is on them that much of our discussion will concentrate, since they seem to provide the most plausible justifications for the probation service (as an agency inherently concerned with crime and criminal justice) to work in a non-individualised way. Another theme which appeared in Henderson's work and which has been explicitly developed in subsequent thinking is that of inter-agency co-operation, which is held to be essential in crime prevention and support for victims. This too will therefore be one of the main themes of this chapter.

Crime prevention and communities: developments in theory and policy

In this section we want to suggest that, while there are still no easy answers, some recent developments in criminology and criminal justice policy can be helpful in pointing to possible ways forward. Firstly, the 1980s saw important advances in knowledge about patterns of crime and criminality in Britain. Most importantly, the successive British Crime Surveys (Hough and Mayhew, 1983 and 1985; Mayhew *et al.*, 1989) have shed light on the 'dark figure' of unreported and unrecorded crime, at least in respect of personal victimisation. Supported by a number of local studies, the national surveys have shown, for example, that both crime and victimisation are highly concentrated in particular neighbourhoods; that those who are most likely to commit crimes are also most likely to become crime victims; that over 90 per cent of crime is never 'solved', in the sense that an individual is officially identified as responsible (and that only 3 per cent of crime leads to a conviction in court (see Barclay, 1991)); that Afro-Caribbean and Asian people are more likely than whites to be victims of crimes against the person; and that the public at large, and recent victims in particular, do not want to see harsher sentencing than the courts currently impose. These findings have important implications for crime prevention initiatives and efforts to respond helpfully to the needs of victims, which we discuss later in this chapter.

Secondly, more local and focused studies have increased our knowledge about the senses in which crime is a problem of communities, not just of individuals. Crime and victimisation are very unevenly distributed in society, and are disproportionately problems for the poor and disadvantaged (Forrester *et al.*, 1988; 1990; Sampson, 1991). This will hardly come as news to probation officers, but for much of the 1980s it was politically imperative for the government to deny that there was any connection between social deprivation and crime. There are signs, however, that the agenda for the 1990s may be different; the maps of crime and poverty fit each other too well for it to be possible to argue that crime is purely opportunistic or situationally specific, or that poverty and discrimination are irrelevant to thinking about its causation.

While the long-term statistical links between crime and general levels of economic activity are complex, the most sophisticated British analysis (Field, 1990) found that property crime tended to increase in periods of decreased consumption, while rises in violent crime were associated with periods of economic boom (probably because, with more money to spend, people go out more, drink more, and therefore spend more time in situations in which they are at risk of assault). Field also found, however, a strong association between unemployment and violent crime; and the cohort study of Farrington *et al.* (1986) provides direct evidence that unemployed people are more likely to become involved in crime than their working counterparts. It appears that while a high level of crime is not necessarily associated with long-term poverty, a sudden worsening of the economic conditions of those who are already vulnerable to changes in the labour market is associated with a higher risk of criminal behaviour.

One relevant message to be drawn from this work on the association between crime, poverty and neighbourhood deprivation is that offenders are not somehow set apart from the communities on which (supposedly) they prey, but are themselves members of those communities. It is politically convenient and comforting to make a sharp distinction between virtuous (or at least innocent) victims and vicious offenders, but such a distinction cannot be empirically supported in the case of many who live in an environment of chronic deprivation and disorder. Smith (1986) describes the idea of a clear dividing line as 'a figment of the political imagination and a sop to social conscience', and Peelo *et al.* (1992), in their graphic case studies of offenders as victims, show how the experience of victimisation can contribute both immediately and over the long term to an increased likelihood of offending. Clearly not all victims are offenders, and in many cases, especially where there is a large power imbalance between offender and victim, such as racial attacks and harassment, and violence against women and children, it would be nonsense to talk of the roles as inter-changeable. Nevertheless, it is important to remember that many people supervised by the probation service are also victims: the burglar is burgled, the attacker attacked; and this pattern is maintained, and probably exaggerated, when the offender is sent to prison. Equally, we should remember that among the statuses occupied by offenders is that of 'law-abiding citizen'.

We need, then, to see offenders not as predatory outsiders or the hyenas of the Home Office's 1992 campaign on 'autocrime', but as fellow citizens and participants in local communities. This perspective is part of what Currie (1988) described as 'Phase 2' of thinking about community crime prevention, and developments in crime prevention theory and practice are the next topic we want to discuss in setting the context in which the probation service will need to pursue the aim of greater community involvement. Currie argues that in 'Phase 1' the emphasis was on communities defending themselves against offenders who posed a threat from the outside. The favoured strategies were neighbourhood watch, opportunity reduction and attempts to increase 'defensible space'. More recently (from the late 1980s), the limitations of these approaches have become apparent. This is partly a matter of empirical evidence about their effectiveness: neighbourhood watch, for example, has produced results that can most kindly be described as 'mixed' (Bennett, 1990; Husain and Bright, 1990); and even apparently straightforward attempts to reduce opportunities for crime by 'target-hardening' may have disappointing results (for example, Hope, 1985). The problems, however, are also theoretical: these approaches depend on a view of 'community' which is arguably naive, idealistic and empirically wrong.

In Phase 1, community is viewed, essentially, as a set of virtuous attitudes and beliefs; communities are seen as united, homogeneous and harmonious, with a well-defined sense of their collective interests. In Phase 2, the real nature of many so-called communities is more clearly recognised: far from being cosy havens of consensus, actual communities (or neighbourhoods) are split and conflict-ridden, along lines of class, race, age and other divisions. This is likely to be especially true of areas in which crime problems are most acute. Hence the uncomfortable finding that neighbourhood watch tends to be most successful in areas which need it least: where there already exists a sense of community, of citizen participation in activities to promote a common good, and of practical neighbourly concern (Rosenbaum, 1988). Resting on a naive view of community, neighbourhood watch depends in areas which lack these desirable characteristics on what Rosenbaum calls the Implant Hypothesis, that 'citizen participation, and eventually, informal social control mechanisms, can be 'implanted' from outside' (p. 141). The message of the research is that this approach – encouraging neighbours to watch each other's property, and to be wary of strangers – is likely to fail on its own; it needs to be accompanied by a range of other community development strategies, reflecting the real complexity of disadvantaged communities.

At one level this message may seem depressing: things are harder than we hoped. On the other hand, in so far as Phase 2 thinking is more realistic about high crime communities and their problems, it should encourage the development of more realistic strategies. By recognising that those who commit crimes are often members of the communities within which they offend, and insisting on the relevance of social and economic factors as the material basis of community life, Phase 2 allows a widening of the agenda to include issues treated as irrelevant in the simplifications of Phase 1. Questions of housing, employment, education, racial discrimination, the oppression of women by men, economic marginalisation and impoverishment again become relevant in thinking about crime prevention; it becomes possible to think again about the causes of crime, instead of treating it as a more-or-less random product of opportunities for its commission. This environment, we suggest, is likely to be more hospitable to the presence of the probation service than an approach to crime prevention solely reliant on increasing surveillance and physical security. The move from Phase 1 to Phase 2 is roughly that from 'situational' to 'social' crime prevention, the former concerned purely with the physical aspects of prevention, the latter with social factors associated with crime. While in practice successful crime-prevention initiatives are likely to combine elements of both, we think the distinction remains a useful one, not least for identifying the aspects of crime prevention to which the probation service can most usefully contribute.

Another well-established but still useful distinction is that between primary, secondary and tertiary levels of crime prevention (Brantingham and Faust, 1976). Primary prevention is universalist, in that it entails provision for the community as a whole. It is concerned with identifying social, economic and environmental circumstances which may tend to facilitate or encourage crime, and working to reduce their crime-producing potential; it often entails a broad-based programme of social or environmental improvement, or community development. Secondary prevention relates to work with specific groups or individuals (usually young) who have been identified as at risk of becoming offenders; it has often been thought to carry with it the risk of stigmatising those labelled 'at risk' and drawing them unnecessarily into the criminal justice system (a view particularly influential among juvenile justice practitioners), but recent developments in youth social work, which we discuss later in this chapter, suggest that this process is not inevitable (Blagg and Smith, 1989). Tertiary prevention refers to work with known offenders. The probation service can in this sense quite legitimately claim that it has always been involved in crime prevention, through its work with people on supervision; and the prison service could say the same. But for the purposes of this discussion, which deals with the service's work with communities rather than with individuals, 'crime prevention' means work at the primary and secondary levels.

A role for the probation service?

While it is true that interest in crime prevention developed in the mid-1970s partly as a result of exaggerated pessimism about the feasibility of effective correctional work with labelled offenders, and a resulting despair about identifying the causes of crime (Mayhew *et al.*, 1976), the shift of focus away from the treatment of identified offenders and on to crime prevention has been seen by some commentators as beneficial for the quality of debate and the development of policy. One of those mainly responsible for it, Mary Tuck, who was Head of the Home Office's Research and Planning Unit for much of the 1980s, has argued that this 'paradigm shift' has allowed a helpful broadening of the agenda of criminal justice debates, away from narrow concerns with punishment and sentencing to the more important issues of prevention (Tuck, 1987; see also Harris, 1989). Bearing in mind what a small proportion of criminal acts lead to a conviction, it is hard to disagree that these issues are more important from the perspective of society as a whole, and difficult to maintain that the probation service should not seek to contribute to the new developments in thinking and practice. It is less easy, however, to specify just what this contribution should be.

The Home Office itself has given some ambiguous messages to the probation service about its role in crime prevention. The 1984 Statement of National Objectives and Priorities appeared to stress (though in rather vague terms) the need to make better use of community resources through inter-agency co-operation rather than crime prevention specifically (Henderson, 1987). Since then, however, most Home Office pronouncements on community involvement, while remaining tentative about how large a role the probation service should play, have been clear that a principal aim of this should be crime prevention, the other being work with victims of crime. As suggested earlier, it is hard to see how these could fail to provide the main justifications for non-individualised, community-based practice for the probation service. Rule 37 of the 1984 revision of the Probation Rules incorporates both aims:

It shall be the duty of a probation officer to participate in such arrangements concerned with the prevention of crime or with the relationship between offenders and their victims or the community at large as may be approved by the probation committee on the advice of the chief probation officer.

The Home Office has been clear in broad policy statements that crime prevention should be part of the work of the probation service, while being less clear about what this might entail in practice. The service has been represented on the Home Office's Standing Conference on Crime Prevention since 1987 (Geraghty, 1991), and the Green and White Papers of 1988 and 1990 (Home Office, 1988; 1990a; 1990b) contained (among much else) some messages of encouragement. The 1990 White Paper stated that 'the inter-agency work of the probation service on crime prevention should grow' (para. 3.9), and its Green companion said that the service 'must gear its work more and more towards crime prevention in the broadest sense' (para. 3.2). The slightly later paper on 'Partnership in Crime Prevention' (Home Office, 1990d) was not, however, explicit about what the precise role of the service should be. Despite the use of the term 'partnership' (which is calculated to engender feelings almost as warm as the term 'community'), the emphasis in this document was very firmly on the leading role of the police; while it recognised more clearly than the Home Office had done before that local authorities could and should be involved in crime prevention strategies, its most specific suggestion for probation was that officers could make available to the police their 'local knowledge of specific factors which have contributed to crime' (para. 3.4). This echoed a point made in an early and helpful discussion of the contribution probation might make (Laycock and Pease, 1985), but it hardly suggested that crime prevention should develop as a distinctive area of practice within probation, and fell short of the role the service was already playing.

A more general difficulty for probation services trying to decide what priority should be given to crime prevention or other work in the community is that they are being told to expand their work in this field at the same time as they are being told rather more insistently to concentrate on other things, especially the provision of effective supervision in the community. Community involvement has the air of an afterthought in many Home Office statements, whose main thrust is the need to target resources on those who, the government hopes, will be sentenced to punishment in the community rather than to custody. This emphasis on tightly focused work, which also appears throughout the influential report on probation of the Audit Commission (1989), cannot easily be made to accommodate crime prevention, which, especially in its more 'social' forms, is necessarily more diffuse (because it is not aimed at known individuals) and unlikely to be capable of demonstrating 'value for money' quickly, if at all. According to Geraghty (1991), this sense of incompatibility is more of a problem for practitioners and middle managers than for headquarters staff – and it is not in headquarters that the work of community crime prevention needs to take place.

In this section we have outlined the development of thinking on crime prevention in recent years, and suggested that the move towards a more social, community-based perspective has helped to clarify the role that probation officers might have in crime prevention initiatives. We have shown that the service has on the whole responded positively to official encouragement to engage in work in the community, but that both the response and the encouragement have been uneven. In our view, the value of social justice remains important for the probation service if it is not to find itself solely occupied with the enforcement of community penalties, and the effort to find a viable form of work in the community should therefore be maintained. In the next section we turn to examples of community crime prevention in probation practice.

Probation crime prevention practice

In a recent, empirically-based study, Jane Geraghty, an Assistant Chief Probation Officer who was seconded for three years from the start of 1989 to the Home Office Crime Prevention Unit, found that in the four areas studied about two-thirds of all community initiatives in which probation officers were involved belonged to the level of primary prevention, in that they were aimed at the general population in a given neighbourhood; and that only just over one-third of all activity had crime prevention as its central focus (Geraghty, 1991). Nearly half of all the work identified had crime prevention as an additional, rather than a central, aim – for example, work with victims, in child protection and with black communities; and, in the category of secondary prevention, work on addictions, homelessness, and the protection of vulnerable young people. The distinction between work centrally focused on crime prevention and work where this is an additional or even an incidental aim is an important one whose implications are worth exploring.

As we noted above, secondary crime prevention has often been focused on young people identified as 'at risk' of offending, and as such it has aroused suspicion among practitioners. Among juvenile justice workers, the 'new orthodoxy' of the 1980s was that work needed to be tightly focused on those at immediate risk of custody or care (Thorpe *et al.*, 1980); any preventive work (certainly at the secondary level) was regarded as likely to be ineffective and, worse, liable to stigmatise young people and draw them unnecessarily into the criminal justice or care systems (in which it was assumed that the outcomes would inevitably be harmful). From the mid-1980s on, however, emerging ideas on 'youth social work' (Paley *et al.*, 1986) began to suggest that it was possible to work usefully with groups – rather than individuals – defined as vulnerable not just to offending but to other forms of social disadvantage, in ways which avoided the negative labelling process which had been feared (for a discussion of this work, see Blagg and Smith, 1989). A later account of projects with which the Home Office-supported organisation Crime Concern has been involved confirms that 'youth crime prevention' need not entail close links with the formal criminal justice system; the projects described by Findlay *et al.* (1990) – of which more later – aim at a range of social benefits, among which crime prevention is only one.

It is still reasonable to ask at what age secondary crime prevention should start, and there is evidence that supports continued suspicion of the 'catch 'em young' position, however superficially plausible and politically appealing this may be. In a review of what is known about criminal careers and their implications for prevention, much of it based on the Cambridge longitudinal study with which he has been involved for many years, Farrington (1990) suggests that it is possible to predict the likelihood of future conviction with a fair degree of accuracy by identifying salient characteristics of 8- to 11-year-old boys' behaviour and backgrounds. From his evidence, however, future offending is more likely to be prevented by intervention to improve children's prospects within the education system, through some form of 'Head Start' programme, and perhaps by advice and support on parenting skills, than by attempts to deal directly with signs of impending delinquency. The factors identified in the Cambridge research as early predictors of offending – difficulties at school, behavioural problems, erratic parenting, overcrowding at home at so on – are also predictors of other problems in later life; and the evidence suggests that the probation service's traditional concentration on older age groups is empirically justified; other social agencies are better placed than probation to intervene at this early stage.

The probation service has, however, played an active part in supporting the kind of projects described by Findlay *et al.* (1990) in their guide to good practice in youth crime prevention. Echoing King's (1988) distinction between project-driven and programme-driven approaches, they argue that work should be long-term and co-ordinated rather than a series of short-term projects; that it should entail consultation with young people and provide opportunities for them to participate in relevant decisions; that it should recognise that agencies may have to change, as well as young people; and that it should have a practical commitment to equal opportunities. Their case studies cover neighbourhood-based, issue-based and police initiatives in conjunction with local schools. In neighbourhood-based work, the pattern is usually for a small team to support local voluntary effort under the guidance of an inter-agency management committee, using approaches such as detached youth work, youth club work, advocacy on behalf of young people and local groups, and the provision of advice and resource centres. In issue-based work a similar range of methods is used to focus on specific problems such as substance abuse and racial abuse and attacks.

In both types of initiative the probation service has tended to be involved through representation on the management com- mittee rather than in direct work with young people or local groups working on their behalf; but as more officers have been appointed with a specific crime prevention brief, the service has become more involved at the front line, usually alongside youth and community workers. The Crime Concern authors, in a survey in early 1989, received information on 250 projects in England, Wales and Scotland, suggesting a wealth of local activity. In many areas, however, they found that there was no corporate strategy on youth crime prevention; that key agencies had no defined policy; that co-operation between agencies was often poor or absent; and that work was often hampered by uncertainties about funding and unreasonable pressure to show quick results. In arguing for crime prevention policy to develop a 'youth dimension', they suggest that the probation service is one of the agencies which needs to be centrally involved.

Geraghty (1991) provides more direct evidence of what probation services are doing in crime prevention initiatives, and not only those with an emphasis on young people. As mentioned above, she found that senior management were clearer than practitioners that crime prevention ought to be part of the main- stream of probation activity (a discrepancy which the ideas advanced in the next chapter might help to reduce). Headquarters staff argued that the service should encourage a view of crime prevention which emphasised the reintegration of offenders into their communities rather than their exclusion (a decidedly 'Phase 2' perspective); that the service's knowledge of patterns of crime should inform local initiatives and wider policy debates (for instance, on the likely impact on offending of changes in social security entitlements); and that the service could act as a catalyst in creating inter-agency groups to work on a co-ordinated approach to crime problems. In addition, crime prevention projects were seen as suitable for community service labour.

Geraghty describes a number of projects in some detail, and it may be useful to give some examples here, to indicate the range of work which can take place under the 'crime prevention' rubric, as well as the organisational and financial complexity of some arrangements. The 'Birmingham Wheels Project' was originally a probation initiative, with staff mainly funded by the Manpower Services Commission Community Programme. Sited on derelict land, it aimed to provide an opportunity for disadvantaged young people to gain legitimate excitement and pleasure from 'wheeled vehicles' (anything from skateboards to cars). Additional aims were to encourage an interest in driving and car maintenance, to promote high standards of behaviour on the roads, and to use the wheel-based activities as an opportunity to set a good example of considerate, responsible conduct. Environmental improvement was a welcome by-product. The project has now been handed over to the Birmingham Wheels Company, a charity whose Board of Directors consists of city councillors and members of the probation committee. Its objectives make clear that it aims to benefit both sentenced offenders and those 'who are in or exposed to moral danger including the risk of becoming involved in the commission of crimes' (Geraghty, 1991, p. 26).

'The Cave', also in Birmingham, is housed in a former cinema acquired by the probation service in 1982. The project now has 'mainstream' funding, but was initially financed by an Inner City Partnership with Arts Council support. It was intended as an arts-based centre for offenders and those at risk, as well as an intermediate treatment resource, a 'minority arts' centre, and a general community response. The focus of The Cave's work, like that of the Handsworth Cultural Centre established earlier, is with Afro-Caribbean and Asian people who, it is recognised, have often felt alienated from conventional forms of probation practice. A 1987 internal report on its work quoted by Geraghty speaks of the importance of 'a sense of belonging' as a contribution to 'greater social cohesion'.

The Hillsleigh Road Project in Cowgate, Newcastle upon Tyne, is an example of a probation service effort to raise its profile and improve its service on a particular estate. Starting with Manpower Services Commission finance, it has been funded by the probation service since 1983. Its focus is on groupwork available to the community as a whole, but focused on special interests – hence Geraghty reports (p. 31) the existence of an unemployed group, boys', girls' and women's groups, a sewing club and a lunch club. The project also aims to link offenders with other local facilities, to demonstrate the probation service's commitment to the estate, and to strengthen links between probation and other agencies.

A different approach to crime prevention, and one which many probation officers might find more familiar, is illustrated by the Wayside Day Centre, also in Newcastle. This probation initiative, intended to tackle the links between homelessness and offending, is a voluntary drop-in centre catering for vulnerable people, many of them homeless, who have fallen through the net of other welfare services. The centre provides a comfortable, safe environment in which bizarre behaviour can be tolerated and then controlled; it encourages relationships with staff and other centre users, and the development of constructive interests; it acts as a referral and advice centre on such problems as homelessness, poverty, drink or drug abuse, and mental and physical illness; and provides advice and practical help on resettlement into independent living. Many of the centre's users are extremely disturbed and, in conventional terms, difficult, and some have committed serious offences of sex and violence; but many are also victims, vulnerable to abuse or exploitation by the more socially competent and successful; and the centre is also sometimes the first refuge for women and their children in flight from an abusive relationship.

From these examples and others given by Geraghty, and from our own experience and observation, crime prevention in the community requires probation officers to have skills which are distinct from (and not necessarily co-existent with) those which are needed for structured, clearly defined work with offenders. For example, the Wayside Centre and similar projects elsewhere require staff who can work in an open, casual environment with people who are often unpredictable, potentially violent, drunk, loud, demanding and disturbing. As well as the skills needed in direct contact with service users, all these projects also require probation staff to be able to liaise effectively with other agencies, to articulate a distinctive probation view to people who may not be easily persuaded, to research local needs and resources, and to handle a variety of meetings appropriately. While the projects described above all have reasonably secure funding, this is not always the case, and fund-raising may be among the skills demanded of a probation officer specialising in crime prevention. It should be remembered also that much crime prevention work consists not of direct work with offenders or those at risk, but of sitting (and preferably more than that) on committees, panels, bureaux and inter-agency forums.

Making sense of inter-agency co-operation

One consistently recurring theme in recent thinking about criminal justice generally, and crime prevention in particular, has been the need for inter-agency co-operation. The agencies and professions which make up the 'system' (if it can be called that) are continually being encouraged to see themselves and their role in relation to the whole. This applies not only to the probation service but also, for example, to sentencers, as in the Woolf Report's insistence (Home Office, 1991b) that they ought to know about conditions in local prisons before sending anyone to them. The Home Office has, since the autumn of 1989, organised a series of high-level national and regional conferences in which representatives of the various agencies and professions – police, probation, prisons, the crown prosecution service, social services departments, justices' clerks, judges, magistrates, solicitors and barristers, along with representatives of the voluntary sector, including Victim Support – have been brought together to explore possibilities of improved co-operation. The Home Office Annual Report for 1991 (Home Office, 1992e) states that the purpose of these conferences is to encourage 'a greater mutual understanding of their [the different agencies'] problems and priorities; a stronger sense of collective purpose and shared objectives; and a deeper understanding of the wider social, economic and political contexts in which the services operate'.

It is not only the Home Office which has stressed the centrality of inter-agency co-operation to the development of effective strategies to deal with crime problems. In a recent textbook on the place of the probation service within an integrated criminal justice system, Harris (1992) argues that inter-agency working should displace direct work with offenders as the core concern of the service. Drawing on the experience of joint work in child protection, Harris suggests that it is possible for agencies with distinct ideologies and traditions to work productively towards a common end. In our view, he too readily glosses over some of the difficulties which are often encountered in practice and which we explore below – as, inevitably, exhortations from the Home Office also do. The importance of inter-agency working in the field of youth crime prevention specifically has also been consistently stressed by NACRO (1991b; 1991c), with a more realistic appreciation of the gap between aspiration and achievement.

Problems in practice

The most substantial research on inter-agency working in criminal justice, which included a focus on crime prevention, was completed in late 1987, but still appeared relevant to many participants in the system in 1992, judging by the response to the summary of it presented at the regional Home Office conferences by one of the present writers. The research, aspects of which are reported in Blagg *et al.* (1988), Sampson *et al.* (1988; 1991), Pearson *et al.* (1989) and Sampson and Smith (1992), focused on the relations between the police, the probation service and social services departments, and their interactions with a range of local community groups. Crime prevention was one of the topics examined in the research, which was conducted at a number of sites in London and in 'Milltown', in the north of England. Across the various topics considered and the different sites, the authors identified a number of common issues and problems in inter-agency work. Perhaps the most fundamental was that the agencies which are expected to co-operate do not start as equals; some 'are more powerful than others (and most are more powerful than the probation service)' (Sampson and Smith, 1992, p.106). The authors also identified problems of confidentiality (what information to share, and with whom), and of levels and styles of representation (for example, at what level in the various organisational hierarchies should inter-agency communication take place? What are the advantages and disadvantages of formal and informal styles of communication?) which they believed had been neglected in previous thinking about inter-agency work. They also (especially Sampson *et al.* 1991) highlighted the importance of gender relations in shaping patterns of inter-agency communication, arguing that the absence of any attention to questions of sex and gender in most writing about organisations was a serious gap when considering, for example, relations between the police and social workers.

The researchers argued that attempts to increase inter-agency co-operation should start from the recognition that structural – not merely personal or cultural – conflicts exist between the agencies involved, reflecting different and not necessarily compatible aims, priorities and interests; and that these 'should not be regarded as unequivocally a "bad thing"' (Sampson and Smith, 1992, p. 106). The criminal justice system has, after all, a number of built-in 'checks and balances' which are designed to prevent the domination of one set of interests, and it would be surprising, and worrying, if probation officers, social workers and police officers (not to mention crown prosecutors, judges and solicitors) always agreed on everything. The researchers found that, while there were important local variations in inter-agency relations, the most powerful agency in crime prevention was generally the police, with local authority housing departments also having an important say in the direction of estate-based projects. The power of these agencies rested on the resources at their command and on their apparently superior knowledge of local crime problems. Thus on local crime prevention panels and forums it was the police who tended to set the agenda and define what the problems were, and had a freedom denied to other participants to work outside the inter-agency framework when they wished.

In considering probation officers' involvement in community crime prevention, Sampson and Smith (1992) suggested that, as soon as officers saw community involvement as something more than a means of improving their service to individual clients, they ran into a number of uncertainties. One was about the nature of 'community': were offenders in any useful sense members of it, or had they been effectively excluded and alienated? And what, if you managed to find 'the community', should you do then? Was the work of the probation service not inherently based on concern for individuals – in contrast with the police, who were inherently concerned with the community as a whole? Officers were also often unclear on what it meant to represent the service in a 'community' setting (as Geraghty (1991) found in her later research), when it might be difficult to reconcile the needs and interests of vulnerable and marginalised people with those of the respectable community. Hence:

> I think that for things like management committees and tenants' associations, for example, we have to ask 'What the hell are we here for?'. We have to be sure why we're there, otherwise we get demoralised, challenged without having anything to offer, even angry. (Senior probation officer quoted in Sampson and Smith, 1992, p.107)

Confidentiality was often hard to reconcile with non-individualised forms of work, especially in respect of communication with the police. The 'problem families' or 'criminal elements' who are often the centre of discussion in local crime prevention forums are likely to be clients of the probation service, which places officers who are members of these groups in an awkward position. Relations with the police were not helped by the tendency of probation clients to tell their officers alarming tales of police malpractice. These could undermine trust and respect, even if officers did not believe everything they were told; and the apparently routine experience of sexual harassment by police officers of women social workers and probation officers, especially in the court setting, had a similar effect.

Despite their concern with the factors which may complicate inter-agency working, and make it harder in practice than it sounds in Home Office circulars, Sampson and Smith come to relatively optimistic conclusions about the feasibility of a crime prevention role for the probation service, largely because they recognise that there have been shifts in thinking about the issue since the time of their research, along the lines discussed earlier in this chapter. The police are no longer so narrowly wedded to a hard-nosed, situational, opportunity-reduction approach, as the social and economic factors associated with crime have come to be more generally accepted. And in trying to identify the practical lessons to be drawn from the research, and from later analysis of the questionnaire responses of participants at the regional criminal justice conferences, Smith (1992) suggests a number of factors associated with success and failure in crime prevention and other inter-agency initiatives. These are, interestingly, similar to the factors listed by Geraghty (1991) as characteristics of 'focused' and 'unfocused' crime prevention work. A consistent finding is that initiatives are most likely to succeed when they are clearly targeted at a specific, feasible objective (it is not enough to set up an inter-agency group to tackle 'crime prevention' without specifying in more detail what crime, when, where and so on). Successful initiatives are also characterised by: commitment by all parties involved; adequate resources and information; authoritative support from agency managers and policy makers; good planning and preparation;

common aims clearly understood by all; and some means of monitoring progress and evaluating outcome (which is impossible unless the aims of the initiative are well defined).

In the absence of one or more of these predictors of success, inter-agency work is likely to fail. And, while it is important to be realistic about the problems for practice which it presents, it is also clear that the probation service cannot avoid being increasingly involved in work which entails close contact with other agencies. This message permeates the 1991 Criminal Justice Act and the thinking which led to it; it is a central theme of the Woolf Report, whose first recommendation was the establishment of a national Criminal Justice Consultative Council (set up in January 1992) which would bring together different interests and agencies at the highest level; it is inherent in the Home Office's (1990c) proposals for 'partnership' between the probation service and the 'independent sector'. These developments promise an ever-higher profile for inter-agency work, and will raise some new issues which will need to be resolved (Smith *et al.*, 1993).

It is important that probation officers' (and others') experience of inter-agency working should be positive and productive; if, instead, experience of failure leads to disillusionment and cynicism, the principle will fall into disrepute, and low expectations will lead to low levels of commitment, and inevitably to further failure. For the probation service, there are implications for training and for management, which are discussed in the next chapter, if the service is to become the open, responsive organisation it needs to be to work constructively with other agencies.

The probation service and victims of crime

So far in this discussion victims have been a rather shadowy presence, although it might be thought obvious that they should be at the centre of any crime prevention initiative. We want now briefly to review the experience of the probation service in work related to victims, and to explore ways of linking efforts to support victims with crime prevention and other community-based work. We will argue that while victims and offenders cannot be neatly categorised into two mutually exclusive groups, there are inherent tensions for the probation service, which is traditionally and properly seen as concerned with offenders and their interests, in trying also to work in the interests of victims. For example, as Rock (1990) shows, it took some time for the service to find a role in victim support which was perceived by representatives of victims as helpful and appropriate; the infant victim support movement feared, and successfully resisted, being taken over by the probation service, which would have meant a distortion of its aims and priorities. The background supportive role which the service now characteristically plays, making its knowledge and experience available when required, represents a successful resolution of potential inter-agency conflict, and a realistic acceptance of the tension between victims' and offenders' interests.

Mediation and reparation

The tension was certainly apparent in the various attempts in the mid-1980s to bring victims and offenders together following an offence in the hope that, through mediation, some form of reconciliation or reparation might be accomplished (see Smith *et al.*, 1988 for an account of one scheme, and Marshall and Merry, 1990, for a review of research on four others). These projects had their origins in a sense of dissatisfaction with the bureaucratic processes of the formal criminal justice system, which were seen as denying victims any opportunity to participate in the resolution of an offence (Christie (1977) was a major influence), and in the success of the then National Association of Victim Support Schemes (now Victim Support) in raising the needs and interests of victims as an issue susceptible to practical reforming action, rather than political exploitation (Rock, 1990). The NAVSS placed victims firmly on the agenda of criminal justice debates, and the 1990 'Victim's Charter', precursor of the Citizen's Charter, is a sign of the government's continued commitment (at least at the level of political rhetoric) to taking victims seriously.

The projects, especially those which were 'court-based' (that is, operated in a context in which the offender was being prosecuted) demonstrated a number of positive achievements. They showed that victim/offender mediation is feasible, that many victims welcome an opportunity to meet 'their' offender, and that most of those who do so are satisfied with the experience. The notion of some form of reparation, emotional and social as well as purely material, seems to be in line with intuitive ideas of natural justice. As Marshall and Merry (1990, p. 239) note, the projects also showed that

> the community has a role to play in dealing with crime, enabling society to construct a positive experience to comple-ment what is, perhaps inevitably, the emotively negative impact of the law alone.

Mediation also seemed to affect offenders more, and more positively, than appearing in court, increasing their sense of responsibility and understanding of the impact of their offence rather than simply punishing and condemning. Sentencers, in turn, were generally willing to take account of what mediation had achieved and reflect this in their decisions.

With this positive evaluation, it is perhaps surprising that activity in victim/offender mediation has declined (along with governmental enthusiasm) since the projects described Marshall and Merry reached the end of their period of central funding in 1987. These authors identify a number of difficulties which may account for the failure of mediation to develop as its advocates hoped it would. The projects encountered, in varying degrees, operational problems over referrals (project workers had a constant struggle to get enough cases in which to attempt mediation); timing (mediation had to move not at its own pace but at that of the other agencies involved in processing cases through court); preparation for mediation and follow-up after it; and resources (Marshall and Merry comment – p. 244 – that 'victim/offender mediation, if it is to be principled and beneficial and not just a gimmick, cannot be obtained "on the cheap"'). Bearing in mind that these projects received special Home Office funding, the resource problem might seem a serious one for the probation service, though Marshall and Merry's assessment is that court-based schemes can 'pay their way' if notional savings arising from a reduction in prison sentences are taken into account.

More fundamentally, the schemes found it difficult to maintain their basic principles of restorative justice in the context of a criminal justice system wedded to more traditional concepts of the issues raised by an offence as an addition to, rather than as a substitute for, the normal legal processes. It was also difficult for schemes to maintain their intended balance between the offender's and the victim's interests: located as they were within criminal justice agencies, and relying on referrals from probation officers or defence solicitors, workers were under constant pressure to give priority to the interests of offenders (a worry voiced by Helen Reeves (1984), the national director of Victim Support). Marshall and Merry suggest that by stressing emotional rather than material reparation, schemes may have risked denying victims what could be regarded as a basic right to have the value of stolen or damaged property restored to them. Finally, although the schemes espoused greater community involvement as an aim in theory, this was barely achieved in practice. Nevertheless, if it were to become the norm that victims of relatively minor crimes should meet 'their' offenders, the fear of the unknown offender which is characteristic of the experience of victims would be reduced, and in the long term one could hope for a change in community attitudes towards crime and offenders, in the direction of reintegration rather than stigmatising exclusion (Braithwaite, 1989). Victim/offender mediation may have lost its 'flavour of the month' status at the Home Office, but it is still practised by probation officers and others, and it seems likely that its strong intuitive appeal will mean that it is not forgotten.

Victim support and crime prevention

The probation service has also participated in work which seeks to unite crime prevention and victim support. Most obviously, there is a link in that crime victims often want practical advice on crime prevention. This was an important element of the successful Kirkholt burglary prevention project (Forrester *et al.*, 1988; 1990): on this estate in Rochdale repeat victimisation was a particular problem, leading to the development of 'cocoon' (small scale) home watch schemes targeted specifically on the most vulnerable properties. The authors argue (1990, p.45) that 'the best predictor of the next victimisation is the last victimisation', and that therefore 'victim support and crime prevention are two sides of the same coin'. The connection between the two was recognised by the establishment in 1988 of a joint 'demonstration project' between the Home Office Crime Prevention Unit and (as it was then) the National Association of Victim Support Schemes on an estate in London. The probation service was among the agencies represented on the project's working group.

The estate chosen for the project presented problems which were more complex than in Kirkholt. Whereas Kirkholt consists mostly of houses rather than flats, has an all-white population, and suffered mainly (as far as was known) from a single type of crime – burglary – the inner city estate on which the CPU/NAVSS project worked consisted of flats, had a racially and socially heterogeneous population, and suffered from a wider variety of offences, including racial attacks and street fights. Fear of crime was high, particularly in relation to personal harm; and women feared sexual attack (Sampson, 1991). Given the range and intensity of the estate's problems, it was decided to adopt a multi-dimensional development approach, in which victim support, neighbourhood watch-type schemes and improved security were intended to be mutually reinforcing. The project supported a number of group activities, such as a community mediation scheme and a 'mothers and toddlers' group, but tensions on the estate, reflected in conflicts within the tenants' association, meant that the workers were always liable to be seen as supporting one faction or another. The tenants' association voted the mothers and toddlers group out of their flat after only seven months, and Sampson comments (p. 30) that the project 'illustrated how crime prevention schemes can increase social conflicts and provide a site for power struggles to be played out'.

Residents' lives

were blighted by social conflicts and tensions. Some of these conflicts reflected divisions between gender, race and age while others were about divergent lifestyles, divisions between the employed and unemployed, disparate values and the use of space on the estate. (p. 32)

The study showed that unless funds were made available for practical improvements in security (which residents could not afford themselves) there was unlikely to be much active support for communal crime prevention activities like neighbourhood watch. In the absence of practical improvements, victims' emotional turmoil or anger continued and contributed to the estate's atmosphere of tension. The project also raised questions about the appropriateness of crime prevention advice: some residents had adopted their own solutions, including the Rottweiler approach; traditional crime prevention advice is irrelevant in the case of personal attacks when the victim and assailant are known to each other (as was generally the case); and in other cases it was hard to think of advice which would not lead to an undesirable curtailment of victims' lifestyles. The project suggested that the success of the Kirkholt scheme might not be easy to replicate elsewhere, especially on estates as internally divided and fearful as this one. Both crime prevention and work with victims need to be adapted to fit local needs and circumstances; and, as with inter-agency working, the result of embarking on community crime prevention with unrealistic expectations is likely to be avoidable disappointment and long-term pessimism.

Conclusions

In this chapter we have suggested that the probation service can and should be involved in work in the wider community as a complement to intensive and focused practice with offenders in court and under supervision. It is not only that this broader engagement with the social context of crime is officially defined as part of the service's role; it is also that in the absence of such a commitment the service risks losing any practical purchase on questions of social justice, and also risks becoming trapped within the bounds of the formal criminal justice system, continually vulnerable to pressure to increase the element of enforcement in its work, at the expense of more positive supportive and developmental elements. We have argued that the main justification for a community perspective in probation is crime prevention and that, in the light of recent advances in criminological knowledge, prevention is intimately linked with help and advice to victims. Developments in policy and practice since the mid-1980s have made crime prevention a more hospitable environment for probation values and interests than it was before, when the emphasis was on the situational, rather than the social, determinants of crime.

In discussing the experience of probation practice in this field, we have suggested that this is most likely to be productive when its aims are most clearly defined and attainable. Work in the community, which necessarily entails work with other agencies, professional and otherwise, demands of probation officers skills and knowledge which are distinct from those needed for day-to-day practice with offenders. It is not surprising that many officers feel uneasy about the relevance of their involvement in work which is inherently less tidy and clear-cut, in its methods and its outcomes, than traditional practice. Effective community crime prevention and victim support are difficult to achieve, especially in the neighbourhoods where, arguably, they are most needed. There is, however, a growing body of knowledge and experience on which probation officers can draw, which we have tried to make accessible in this chapter. We believe that this is especially important in the new environment of the 1991 Criminal Justice Act and the demand for greater coherence and integration in the criminal justice system. The final chapter outlines the kind of organisational culture, critically informed but positive and outward-looking, which will facilitate the pursuit of effectiveness in the service's work in the community.

8

Conclusion: Management and the Pursuit of Effectiveness

Introduction

We have attempted to set out the kind of contribution that the probation service can now make to the criminal justice system, firstly by suggesting strategies through which probation officers can influence sentencers, and secondly by presenting models of effective, anti-discriminatory practice in work with people who offend. In doing so we have quite deliberately placed the work of probation staff in the context of wider concerns about welfare and social problems, and argued that its aim should be to influence systems as well as individuals. Clearly the extent to which that aim can be fulfilled depends in no small measure upon the commitment, skills, knowledge and hard work of individuals engaged in a wide range of tasks, including amongst other things running programmes, advising people, providing practical help, supervising community work, managing information systems and providing clerical services. However, it is likely to be so much wasted effort unless it takes place within a healthy, confident, self-critical and co-operative organisation. In turn those characteristics hinge, not entirely but significantly, around skilled, person-centred leadership, innovative, relevant practice

138

and the evaluation of effectiveness. We devote the main section of this final chapter to an exploration of the keys to organisational health.

The rise of management

In Chapters 1 and 2 we emphasised the growing complexities and heightened challenges which the probation service faces as it undertakes work with more heavily convicted people and deeply entrenched social problems, whilst at the same time being exposed to the increasing glare of both state and public accountability. It has not always been so. The probation service's first sixty or seventy years passed quietly and almost unnoticed by a 'relatively uncritical and supportive' society (Vanstone and Seymour, 1986).

In more recent years, the strange combination of, on the one hand, organisational expansion and innovations in the field of rehabilitative effort, and, on the other, confidence undermined by negative research findings, culminated in the advent of the right-wing political dominance of Thatcherism. Increased interest and control from the centre and its harbinger, the Statement of National Objectives and Priorities (SNOP), were just around the corner. However, the expansion of the probation bureaucracy and the rise to prominence of administration and its attendant increase in regulation had already begun, albeit less intensively, under governments of different political hue. The ten-year period before the Thatcher government witnessed a growth in the probation service hierarchy; a decrease in worker autonomy; the emergence of the concept of teamwork; and a widening gap between headquarters management and the staff engaged in the core tasks of the agency. This significant but piecemeal growth of the bureaucracy, coupled with an increase in tasks and a diversification of practitioner grades, created management problems of control and accountability (Boswell, 1982; Mathieson, 1979; McWilliams, 1987; Raynor, 1985; Vanstone, 1988).

Our description of events in this section has so far had a pejorative tinge. The story of the rise of management is also underpinned by positive action, good intentions and some success in promoting the development of appropriate and potentially effective practice. There has been a very proper concern with accountability and the provision of a service, the quality of which was not dependent simply on the vagaries of individual energy, skills and commitment. However, in our view there have been problems which have been exacerbated firstly, by the 'macho' management style encouraged in the eighties, secondly, by the application of accountancy criteria to a 'people' business, and thirdly, by the contradictions evident in bureaucratic growth (Coulshed, 1990; Hayes, 1989; Lewis, 1991; Humphrey and Pease, 1992). On the one hand staff have listened to messages about innovation, improvement and creativity; and on the other they have often experienced the constraints and poor communication that can occur in an organisation whose bureaucratic structure develops a life and a rationale increasingly remote from the core tasks (in Chapter 5 we referred to research findings which showed that innovative practice can only be sustained in a supportive organisational environment).

The rise of 'managerialism' as a response to the growth of the organisation has been extensively chronicled by Bill McWilliams (1985). We have also given our attention to aspects of that rise but, even so, think it worth pausing to reflect on the role of the senior probation officer (team leader or middle manager) because it provides an interesting perspective on this process and also leads us into some of the issues which we intend to discuss later in the chapter. The Probation Rules of 1927 first permitted the appointment of senior probation officers, but it was not until the 1947 Rules that any clear attempt was made to spell out their duties. Although organisational and managerial functions can be clearly discerned in these rules, the main emphasis is on supervision of and advice to probation officers in relation to their work with clients. These duties were to be undertaken within a service which 'was based on a professional – supervisory – administrative model of organisation geared to the treatment of individual offenders' (McWilliams, 1987). This apparent clarity about the core function of seniors survived from 1947 to the beginning of the seventies. Bill Weston (then a principal probation officer) in referring to the growth of 'management speak', questioned the appropriateness of the term 'management', coming as it does from industry, and emphasised that the responsibility of people in administrative and supervisory positions is 'to ensure that the professional worker is at his [sic] best and is functioning effectively' (Weston, 1973). His concern was that this might be submerged under the increasingly difficult business of ensuring that a complex organisation runs smoothly. The nine broad headings and 94 sub-headings for senior officers' duties in the 1980 Management Structure Review showed how prescient he was.

It has been our intention to suggest that the behaviour, concerns and style of 'middle managers' are useful indicators of the direction being taken by an organisation. We have argued that supervision of practice remains a part of the senior's role but that it has been squeezed by planning and control functions, and that this is characteristic of developments in management practice and style generally within the organisation. Clearly an organisation which is growing in size and which is acquiring a large number of complex tasks needs administration and leadership, and requires systems of supervision and accountability. The choices are about style, emphasis and process. The modern probation service, like other public sector organisations which provide a people-focused service, is in danger of being manoeuvred into inappropriate management practices (McWilliams, 1989). Of course, the national picture is much more complicated than this, and there will be many examples of teams and individuals who strive to work on a collaborative basis. Our purpose is to highlight what can go and is going wrong, to unravel the key issues and to describe a more appropriate model. Three insights into probation services underline the problems which we have described.

Management and change

The first insight comes from David Divine's report following his appointment as a consultant to the West Midlands Probation Service. The background to this is that the Service had acknowledged a critical problem relating to its failure to confirm the appointment of black first-year officers. Management bravely opened its doors and invited Divine into the organisation to investigate. In his report he describes an ethos

> characterised by competitiveness, insensitivity, heavy handedness, a denial of the experience of how staff members feel and think, an unwillingness to acknowledge that a member of staff may have difficulty with a particular activity or simply may be confused about an issue; the routine ill-thought out adherence to platitudes on race and the increasing gulf between rhetoric and practice had led to an unhealthy degree of cynicism, depression, apathy, paralysis in decision-making. In short it is an atmosphere in which real communication cannot take place.   (Divine, 1989, pp. 76–7)

This is not an ethos created by the conspiratorial activities of a group of managers intent on spreading discontent. Indeed, the bringing-in of a consultant is evidence of a desire to respond positively and resolve problems, and in any event most managers share with other staff a desire for stability and low levels of stress in work situations. Such an ethos is much more likely to be the result of a culmination of mistakes, poor decision-making, personalities, vested interest positions, misinterpretations, low skill levels or a lack of properly constituted procedures – the countless subtle processes that together contribute to the effective or ineffective working of any organisation. Divine helpfully spotlights important areas of concern: specifically he cites supervision, clarity of roles and tasks, the induction process and evaluative frameworks as areas in need of ameliorative attention before there is any possibility of resolving the problems surrounding anti-discriminatory practice. Two years later he returned to the department to find out if the original report had any impact and drew the following conclusion: 'The salient concerns which emerged in the original research had been addressed and substantial progress had been made'.

This seems to us to be a good example of the potential for constructive change if the management and practitioners of a service have the courage to invite critical analysis of discrimination within their organisation. The second insight comes from a piece of research into effectiveness measurement in a large probation service, which is based on 35 interviews with all probation service grades, some justices' clerks, magistrates and senior treasury and information officers from inside and outside the area service (Humphrey and Pease, 1992). The researchers reach a number of highly interesting conclusions which not only identify problems but point towards some solutions. In particular they argue that information systems and efficient organisation do not automatically go together, and that such accounting systems can be instrumental either in spreading control over, or giving control to, members of staff. The scenario that emerges from their findings is one in which senior probation officers are becoming further removed from their teams by administrative tasks, with the result that attention to staff's professional development is being squeezed out; and practitioners feel a lack of ownership of gatekeeping processes and targets which emerge from a predominantly top-down process. It suggests that information systems have quite properly been established to illuminate practice outcomes, but without full attention being paid to stimulating a culture in which practitioners value information. Instead of systems of information-gathering empowering practitioners by helping them to more informed and client-relevant practice, they have induced paranoia about being inspected and overseen.

The third example involves an analysis of a process of policy development (in a probation service given the pseudonym, Treen) which culminated in the publication of an objectives booklet in 1985 (May, 1991). The researcher, after a process of familiarisation, spent a period of time in the organisation, during

which he attended meetings, applied a questionnaire and interviewed staff. He draws some general conclusions which are of
particular interest, but firstly let us examine some of his more
specific research findings. Against a background in which staff
were expressing the view that there was a lack of consultation
over policy which was being imposed from above, he asked staff
who they thought had most influence on the formulation of policy. Front line staff and their representative organisation, NAPO,
were seen to have minimal influence, whereas the probation
management (seen as very influential by 63 per cent), Home
Office (48 per cent, very influential) and the government (28.6
per cent, very influential) were seen clearly to be the most
powerful groups. He also asked if staff thought that management
were out of touch with the realities of day-to-day 'front line'
work. A majority (60 per cent) of probation officers thought that
they were. There was a more equivocal answer to the question
about whether management facilitated or directed work, with
43.8 per cent agreeing that they facilitated, 31.4 neither agreeing
nor disagreeing, and 24.8 per cent disagreeing. Interestingly, but
not surprisingly, it seemed that the further away from headquarters in the hierarchy staff were located, the less controlled
they felt.

May's general observations point to a service in which the
headquarters management group was remote; there was confusion
over the purpose of the policy changes; many staff were going
along with the changes because they had to, rather than because
they believed in them; people were overburdened by increased
administration and mounds of paper; and staff thought that an
inappropriate industrial model of management was being applied.

All the situations described create a sense of organisations in
which management and practice are two unrelated activities, thus
making the coherent use of research and information in policy-
making less likely. None of the probation services described is an
extreme; their experience, like that of the other services around
the country, is one of partial success and partial failure. Their
task is to achieve a consistent and progressive improvement
across all areas of practice through a process of collaboration. In

attempting to elaborate the characteristics of such a self-critical, dynamic organisation, it is helpful to consider the two ideal types outlined by one of the present writers (Raynor, 1988).

1. *How things go wrong*
    Ambiguous aims and policy
    New procedures added to old instead of substituting for them (e.g. developing intermediate treatment while continuing to expand residential care; or community service displacing non-custodial rather than custodial sentences)
    Practice routines accommodate to old practices: new labels for old products (e.g. reformatories become 'approved schools' then 'community homes'; or 'after-care' becomes 'through-care')
    Outcomes are often unchanged, often unknown (i.e. not evaluated against goals), often unintended
    Policy is represented as 'near success'.

2. *A problem solving model*
    Policy with clear aims based on explicit values
    Find out what happens now (baseline information)
    Provisional change objectives
    Provisional practice changes
    Monitoring of practices and outcomes (what has really changed?)
    Evaluation in relation to objectives (are these the changes we wanted?)
    Feedback to practice, objectives or policy.

Describing the problem-solving model is the easy bit, but achieving it and the kind of management practice which positively assists the pursuit of effectiveness is dependent on the ethos and culture of the organisation, and those, as we have argued above, are determined by a complex matrix of variables. It is, however, possible to discern the key components of the kind of culture which we argue is a prerequisite for the self critical, problem-solving organisation.

Anti-discriminatory practice

Black people are under-represented in all grades of staff and both black people and women are under-represented in managerial grades. The re-adjustment of this situation through the implementation of equal opportunity policies is essential and can only be achieved through anti-racist practice:

> When anti-racist practice becomes embodied into the fabric of the service, it creates an active strategy which works against all forms of oppression and discrimination.
>
> (Kett *et al.*, 1992)

Anti-discriminatory management is good management practice and each of the components described below flows from that truism.

Leadership style

The kind of style that we envisage derives its rationale from the distributed actions theory as described by Johnson and Johnson (1991). Within this theory leadership can rotate within a group or team according to its particular needs at any one time. The effective designated leader, therefore, eschews rank or status concerns and instead tries to encourage people to work creatively at given tasks. This activity is broken down further into five quite specific leadership practices:

1. Helping to resolve the conflict arising from the desire to retain the status quo and the need to be creative and innovative. Put another way, the leader needs to contribute to an environment which encourages the quest for improvement in knowledge and skills.
2. Inspiring commitment to an agreed vision of what is to be achieved. This will involve opening the door of what is possible by drawing on knowledge and research.
3. Organising staff so that they work collaboratively and as a team in which people feel empowered and valued.

4. Modelling openness, risk-taking and co-operative action – leading by doing and demonstrating that leading is learning as well.
5. Acknowledging and rewarding the efforts and achievements of individuals and groups within the organisation – 'encouraging the heart of staff members'.

Such practices alone will not produce a self-improving organisation. A commitment to working effectively is also required from the workforce generally. It would be naive indeed to assume that the probation service is staffed by people of equivalent commitment, motivation and capacity for work. We should not forget either the arena of industrial relations within which disputes are appropriately handled. There is a shared responsibility for the kind of organisation within which people work. However, style of leadership is probably the single most important ingredient underpinning a 'shared commitment to a high quality of service' (Thomas and Vanstone, 1992). A more visual exposition of the participative style which we are advocating is provided by Adair (see Figure 1).

Figure 1

| Leader-centred teamwork (autocratic style) | | | | | | Group-centred teamwork (participative style) |

Use of authority by leader

Area of freedom for the team

| Leader decides | Leader 'sells' decision | Presents ideas and invites questions | Tentative decision; consults team; leader decides | Presents problems; gets ideas; leader decides | Leader defines limits; team decides | Team given freedom to help define and decide issue |

(*Source*: Adair, 1988, p. 52)

Location and distribution of power and influence

The Thatcher years have witnessed the rise to prominence of the 'right to manage' assumption of almost unfettered managerial power; but this is not necessarily concomitant with influence. Before we go on, it may be useful to clarify the distinction between power and influence. We see power as a capacity to influence or control people which stems from one of six sources:

1. Reward power – derives from an individual's ability to reward behaviour by giving positive results or by removing bad consequences.
2. Coercive power – exists if an individual has the scope to punish people's behaviour and thus control it.
3. Legitimate power – a person will have this because of their nominated position or their special role within the organisation.
4. Referent power – will be conferred on an individual by people who identify with, admire, like or respect her.
5. Expert power – derives from the possession of valued knowledge or skills.
6. Informational power – emanates from the holding of information needed to accomplish particular tasks. (French and Raven, 1959; Raven and Kruglanski, 1970)

Thus in order for a person to exercise influence (as opposed to manipulate or coerce) she needs legitimate power combined with referent, expert and/or informational power. Unfortunately, when things start to go wrong, managers often resort to reward or coercive power. Therefore, distinguishing the appropriate use of power and ensuring its distribution throughout the organisation is vital in order to facilitate achievement and effectiveness. This will require particular attention to the needs of staff who, because of their ethnic origins, gender, sexual preference or position in the hierarchy (clerical staff particularly), are in less powerful positions and/or more vulnerable to the misuse of power.

Looking after staff

Natural support networks will exist in organisations, but sustaining people's energies, commitment and well-being cannot be left to chance. A collaborative leadership style is, as we have described, a cornerstone of a healthy organisation, but in addition there needs to be a number of structures and systems in place.

1. Industrial relations machinery needs to be established for negotiating pay and conditions, promoting health and safety, settling disputes, managing fair disciplinary procedures and combatting discrimination. In a healthy organisation the use of that machinery (except for pay and conditions) ought to occur when other systems have failed.

2. Stress reduction can come from basic caring for people, but also more officially from confidential and independent counselling services provided by the organisation (to which people can go if, for instance, they feel discriminated against or are under personal pressures), and from secure, safe, working environments and procedures.

3. Staff need to be protected, and supported when under pressure, as well as challenged and helped to improve practice. Contentment and effectiveness arc not distant relations, and in addition, therefore, systems need to be established and maintained for supervision and feedback. This can happen most effectively at team level and should rest on team leaders acting as co-ordinators of supervision and not as the traditional sole providers of supervision and support. In this scenario, the team leader's contribution to the supervision agreement, like that of every other team contributor, will be determined by the possession of the required knowledge and skills. For example, consultation aimed at improving a specific aspect of team member A's pre-sentence report writing might be provided by team member B. Supervision agreements would also provide part of the structure and content of the staff development system.

Staff development strategy

Although staff development is a feature of care and support, it warrants space in its own right. Furthermore, clarity of definition is important in relation to staff development, particularly because of the increasing tendency of the probation service to be prescriptive and rule bound. A training model driven purely by organisational need (fitting the worker to the task) becomes more appropriate the more mechanistic an organisation becomes. A more adaptable organisation, within which innovation, flexibility, creativity, collaboration and lateral as well as vertical communication are encouraged, needs a broad-based staff development strategy which takes account of the complexity and dynamic nature of the helping process (McWilliams, 1980; Vanstone, 1987), Such a strategy has to be coherent and relevant to the core tasks of the organisation. It will be partly based on required needs (for example, anti-racist, child abuse and Criminal Justice Act training) which can be met through distinct training activities. The response to wider, desirable developmental needs of teams and team members, whilst remaining congruent with policy, needs to take place within a dynamic culture and to be underpinned by a range of activities which might include peer consultation, team staff development meetings, live supervision and practice rehearsal. Instead of being a marginalised luxurious extra it should be located at the core of day-to-day practice. It should be:

1. relevant to organisational purpose but flexibly orientated towards team needs;
2. structured within a clearly laid out process of supervision and appraisal;
3. concerned with the welfare of staff as well as skills and knowledge;
4. aimed at bringing together individual worth and potential and organisational effectiveness; and it should include a process of induction which prepares new staff for working within the organisation but which at the same time allows

scope for those staff to influence the organisation (induction does not mean indoctrination); and a concern with the values and the language of the organisation (for example, 'helping' as opposed to 'punishing' people).

Conclusion

A healthy organisation which looks after its staff is best placed to exploit the opportunity and nullify the threat which we identified at the beginning of this book. The 1991 Criminal Justice Act is the most significant piece of legislation for the probation service of the past twenty years. It has been accompanied by direct attempts by government to influence the practice of probation officers through national standards. Neither the Act nor the standards have been universally welcomed by probation staff, and there remains a real worry that practice may be constricted by an authoritarian straitjacket. While recognising the force of such anxieties, we have attempted in this book to provide a more optimistic, and we believe realistic, vision of probation work, which is based on care and concern for people who offend and their victims, and on the principles of inclusion rather than exclusion from the community, participation rather than coercion, and demonstrated effectiveness rather than fashion or convenience.

We have argued for a broad definition of effectiveness which encompasses not only reduced rates of offending but also the service's contribution to the amelioration of social problems, and which locates good practice firmly in an anti-discriminatory perspective. Although we have stressed the importance of an organisational commitment to empirically informed practice, we have also warned against a preoccupation with measurement which dehumanises probation activity. If the balance is achieved, it will be by critical practitioners who are interested in questions about why they are doing things, how they are doing them, and whether they are having the desired effect, but who – as Hugman

(1977) urged – remain responsive and flexible human beings rather than simply technicians. It also depends on the service's retaining a commitment to help.

Such sentiments will quite rightly be seen as mere pious intentions if they are not linked to examples from practice such as we have given in this book – instances of innovative, well-organised work which provide templates both for offence-focused and community-development practice. Their common characteristic is the attempt to link practice enhancement to the findings of research; put simply, the staff involved have attempted to find out if what they have tried to do has worked. In doing so they have demonstrated concern for the recipients of their services and increased the likelihood of influencing the criminal justice system as a whole.

In Chapters 3 and 4 we focused on the pre-sentence report as the fulcrum for exerting that influence. It is strategically organised work of the kind we have discussed which creates the opportunity for report writers to exert influence by identifying need and presenting a coherent account of how that need will be met. They may then be able to influence not only sentencing outcomes but, just as importantly, sentencers' understanding of the social context of individual offending.

A service to the courts, to people who offend and to the public which is premised on striving to understand the context of crime and its effects, and rooted in the humanitarian tradition of the probation service, is achievable despite the constraints of the Criminal Justice Act and national standards – to an extent, indeed, because of their positive aspects. It is up to the members of the service to shape the practical effects of the legislation and the standards so that they facilitate rather than hinder appropriate and effective work. Probation staff can be confident in their ability to achieve this, but only if they can practise within an organisation which is curious about its effect on systems and individuals, and characterised by fairness, an even distribution of power, openness, and an informed belief in the possibility of change.

We hope that we have also made clear that we see the probation service as important not only for its contribution to criminal justice but as part of a wider commitment to a society which values and supports individual needs, contributions and potential. Criminal justice policy is often developed and pursued in a way which seems separate from considerations of social justice, but any attempt to deliver meaningful justice for victims and offenders necessarily raises questions about how we respond to poverty, discrimination, suffering and the arbitrary closure of opportunity. A commitment to improving criminal justice is half-hearted and partial unless it is integrated with wider concerns about other forms of unfairness and inequality. We hope that the self-critical and effective probation service of the future will continue to be informed by this wider view of its social commitments.

Appendix

(from Gelsthorpe, Raynor and Tisi, 1992)

QUALITY ASSESSMENT GUIDE
for Pre-Sentence Reports

VERSION 1
(Gatekeeping and Rapid Appraisal)

Read the report and complete Section 1. Then refer back if necessary to complete Sections 2-5. Tick one box for each question, and follow the scoring instructions exactly. Each section carries a different rating – adding up to a total quality rating of 0–40 for the full report.

October 1992

PSR Reader:　　　　　**Writer:**　　　　　**Ref No/Name:**

1. GENERAL ISSUES　　　　　　　　　　　**YES NO**

Is the report logical in structure and
easily read so that the main points can be
grasped on one reading? _____ [ ] [ ]
Is it free from jargon? _____ [ ] [ ]
Is it free from errors of spelling? _____ [ ] [ ]
Is it free from errors of punctuation or grammar? _____ [ ] [ ]
Is it compatible with local guidelines on length and
　　structure or (if no local guidelines) are length and
　　structure acceptable?_____ [ ] [ ]
Does it contain introductory material in compliance
　　with national standards? _____ [ ] [ ]
Does it specify the source of information used?_____ [ ] [ ]
Does it use an appropriate range of sources? _____ [ ] [ ]
Does it indicate verification of key items? _____ [ ] [ ]
　　　　　　　　　　　　　　Total: _____ [ ]

Suggested changes:

Scoring this section: Each **yes** counts as 1 point.
Score for Section 1:　　[ ]

154

2. **CURRENT OFFENCE. Does the report cover:**   **YES NO N/A**

a summary of the offence(s)? _____ [ ] [ ]

the attitude of the offender to the offence? _____ [ ] [ ]

discussion of the context of the offence – including

  aggravating and mitigating circumstances? _____ [ ] [ ]

comment on harm and attitude to victim if

  personal victim? _____ [ ] [ ] [ ]

other factors relevant to an assessment of seriousness? ___ [ ] [ ] [ ]

an explanation by the writer of why the

  offence occurred? _____ [ ] [ ]

                     Total: _____ [ ]   [ ]

Suggested changes:

Scoring this section: Each **yes or N/A** counts as 1 point.
Score for Section 2:   [ ]

3. **RELEVANT INFORMATION ABOUT THE OFFENDER: coverage.**

Does the report: **YES NO N/A**

contain sufficient information about the offender

which is **relevant** to understanding of his/her

offending behaviour or consideration of a

proposed community sentence, concerning:

  social and personal circumstances _____ [ ] [ ]

  personal history_____ [ ] [ ]

  past offending and responses to sentences _____ [ ] [ ] [ ]

comment on future risk of serious harm if

violent or sexual offence?_____ [ ] [ ] [ ]

avoid including information **not relevant** to understanding

  the offence or considering the sentence? _____ [ ] [ ]

clearly explain the relevance of background

  information where necessary? _____ [ ] [ ]

clarify key issues and their significance for

  offending or sentencing? _____ [ ] [ ]

                    Total: _____ [ ]   [ ]

Suggested changes:

Scoring this section: Each **yes or N/A** counts as 1 point.
Score for Section 3:   [ ]

4. **RELEVANT INFORMATION ABOUT THE OFFENDER:**
   language & presentation.

Does the report clearly:	YES	NO
contain unqualified negative statements? _____	[ ]	[ ]
contain belittling or demeaning language?		
(e.g. adults written about as if they are children) _____	[ ]	[ ]
seek to distance or dissociate the report writer from the		
content? (e.g. 'he creates the impression that') _____	[ ]	[ ]
over-emphasize background problems unrelated		
to offence? _____	[ ]	[ ]
fail to cover positive features of offender, e.g. skills,		
resources, community support? _____	[ ]	[ ]
make a generalized plea for leniency unsupported		
by reasons? _____	[ ]	[ ]
contain stereotypical language or negative labelling? ____	[ ]	[ ]
make irrelevant reference to race, gender, age, disability,		
language ability, literacy, religion or sexual		
orientation? _____	[ ]	[ ]
contain evidence of racist assumptions?_____	[ ]	[ ]
contain evidence of sexist assumptions? _____	[ ]	[ ]
fail to take into account offender's experience of		
disadvantage or discrimination where this is relevant		
to offending?_____	[ ]	[ ]
contain evidence of Eurocentric assumptions about		
'normal' family life, culture or child-rearing? _____	[ ]	[ ]
present women primarily as carers for children or		
domestic support of partner? _____	[ ]	[ ]
give general impression of lack of balance or		
objectivity? _____	[ ]	[ ]
Total: _____	[ ]	

```
+-----------------------------------------------------------+
|   Suggested changes:                                       |
|                                                            |
|                                                            |
+-----------------------------------------------------------+
```

Scoring: these are **negative indicators** so count each **yes** as 2 points and subtract the total **yes** points from the maximum section score of 10. If result is below 0, score 0. (Example: one **yes** response gives a score of 8: five or more yes responses give a score of 0).
Score for Section 4:   [ ]

5. CONCLUSION/PROPOSAL   YES NO N/A

Is the proposal clear and unambiguous?_____ [ ] [ ]

Does it follow logically from the body of the report? ____ [ ] [ ]

Does it comply with guidelines (national or local,
as appropriate) regarding the relationship between
proposals and offence seriousness? _____ [ ] [ ]

Are other possible sentences discussed with
reasons for not proposing them?_____ [ ] [ ] [ ]

If proposing a community sentence, does it:

give details of the programme content in
relation to identified needs? _____ [ ] [ ] [ ]

give details of requirements and restrictions on
liberty involved?_____ [ ] [ ] [ ]

discuss the potential effect on the risk of
future offending? _____ [ ] [ ] [ ]

indicate why this particular option or programme
is appropriate?_____ [ ] [ ] [ ]

If not proposing a community sentence, does it:

give reasons based on levels of offence
seriousness? _____ [ ] [ ] [ ]

discuss the risk of future offending?_____ [ ] [ ] [ ]

discuss the effect of likely sentences on the
offender (e.g. the adverse effects of custody)?_____ [ ] [ ] [ ]

discuss the effect of likely sentences on significant
others (eg. the adverse effects of custody)? _____ [ ] [ ] [ ]

                                          Total: _____ [ ]

Suggested changes:

Scoring: Each **yes** counts as 1 point (maximum score of 8).
Score for Section 5:   [ ]

Add the scores for Sections 1,2,3,4,5.
Check the scoring (maximum 40)   **Overall Score:**   [[   ]]

Which sections, if any, have scores below **five**? _____ Date:_____

Bibliography

Adair, J. (1988) *Effective Leadership*, London, Pan.

Ahmed, B. (1990) *Black Perspectives in Social Work*, Birmingham, Venture Press.

Ainley, M. (1979) *An Evaluation of the Impact of Courses Attended on Officers' Subsequent Work* (Personal Social Services Fellowship Paper), Bristol, University of Bristol.

Andrews, D. A., Zinger, I., Hoge, R. D., Bonta, J., Gendreau, P. and Cullen, F. T. (1990) 'Does correctional treatment work? A clinically relevant and psychologically informed meta-analysis', *Criminology*, 28, 369–404.

Audit Commission (1989) *The Probation Service: promoting value for money*, London, HMSO.

Bailey, H. and Purser, B. (1982) *Coventry Alcohol Education Group*, Birmingham, West Midlands Probation Service.

Bale, D. (1987) 'Using a risk of custody scale', *Probation Journal*, 34, 4, 127–31.

Barclay, G. C. (1991) (ed.) *A Digest of Information on the Criminal Justice System*, London, Home Office.

Bean, P. (1976) *Rehabilitation and Deviance*, London, Routledge and Kegan Paul.

Bennett, T. (1990) *Evaluating Neighbourhood Watch*, Aldershot, Gower.

Biestek, F. P. (1961) *The Casework Relationship*, London, Allen and Unwin.

Blagg, H., Pearson, G., Sampson, A., Smith, D. and Stubbs, P. (1988) 'Inter-agency co-operation: rhetoric and reality', in Hope, T. and Shaw, M. (eds) *Communities and Crime Reduction*, London, HMSO.

Blagg, H. and Smith, D. (1989) *Crime, Penal Policy and Social Work*, Harlow, Longman.

Bochel, D. (1976) *Probation and After-Care: Its Development in England and Wales*, Edinburgh, Scottish Academic Press.

Boother, M. (1991) 'Drug misuse: developing a harm reduction policy', *Probation Journal*, 38, 75–80.

Boswell, G. R. (1982) *Goals in the Probation and After-Care Service,* Unpublished PhD thesis, University of Liverpool.

Bottoms, A. E. (1989) 'The concept of intermediate sanctions and its relevance for the probation service', in Shaw, R. and Haines, K. (eds) *The Criminal Justice System: A Central Place for the Probation Service,* Cambridge, Institute of Criminology.

Bottoms, A. E. and McWilliams, W. (1979) 'A non-treatment paradigm for probation practice', *British Journal of Social Work,* 9, 159–202.

Bottoms, A. E. and Stelman, A. (1988) *Social Inquiry Reports,* Aldershot, Wildwood House.

Bottoms, A. E., Brown, P., McWilliams, B., McWilliams, W. and Nellis, M. (1990) *Intermediate Treatment and Juvenile Justice.* London: HMSO.

Braithwaite, J. (1989) *Crime, Shame and Reintegration,* Cambridge, Cambridge University Press.

Braithwaite, J and Pettit, P. (1990) *Not Just Deserts,* Oxford, Oxford University Press.

Brantingham, P. J. and Faust, L. (1976) 'A conceptual model of crime prevention', *Crime and Delinquency,* 22, 284–96.

Broadbent, A. (1989) 'Poor clients: what can I do?' *Probation Journal,* 36, 151–4.

Bryant, M., Coker, J., Estlea, B., Himmel, S. and Knapp, T. (1978) 'Sentenced to social work', *Probation Journal,* 25, 110–114.

Buchanan, J. and Wyke, G. (1987) 'Drug abuse, probation practice and ·the specialist worker', *Probation Journal,* 38, 123–6.

Burney, E. (1985) *Sentencing Young People,* Aldershot, Gower.

Caddick, B. (1991) 'A survey of groupwork in the probation services of England and Wales', *Groupwork* 4, 3, 197–214.

Campbell, D. and Denney, D. (1991) 'The effectiveness of training in the writing of social inquiry reports', *Practice,* 5, 2, 138–52.

Carlen, P. (1989) 'Feminist jurisprudence – or women-wise penology?', *Probation Journal,* 36, 110–14.

Carlen, P. and Worrall, A. (eds) (1987) *Gender, Crime and Justice,* Milton Keynes, Open University Press.

Chapman, T. (1992) 'Creating a culture of change: a report on the evaluation of Turas, an innovative community-based project to reduce "joy-riding" in West Belfast'. Paper given to the 'What works?' conference, Salford.

Chiqwada, R. (1989) 'The criminalisation and imprisonment of black women', *Probation Journal,* 36, 100–5.

Christie, N. (1977) 'Conflicts as property', *British Journal of Criminology*, 17, 1–15.

Christie, N. (1982) *Limits to Pain*, Oxford, Martin Robertson.

Cohen, S. (1985) *Visions of Social Control*, Cambridge, Polity Press.

Coker, J. (1988) *Probation Objectives: A Management View*, Norwich, University of East Anglia.

Collett, S., Evans, M. and Simpson, P. (1990) 'Practice teaching: developing an anti-racist perspective', *Probation Journal*, 37, 112–18.

Commission for Racial Equality (1981) *Probation and After-Care in a Multi-Racial Society*, London, CRE and West Midlands Probation and After-Care Service.

Coulshed, V. (1990) *Management in Social Work*, London, Macmillan.

Curran, J. (1983) 'Social inquiry reports: a selective commentary on the literature', in Lishman, J. (ed.) *Research Highlights 5: Social Work with Adult Offenders*, Aberdeen, Department of Social Work, University of Aberdeen.

Currie, E. (1988) 'Two visions of community crime prevention', in Hope, T. and Shaw, M. (eds) *Communities and Crime Reduction*, London, HMSO.

Dahrendorf, R. (1985) *Law and Order*, London, Stevens & Sons.

Davies, M. (1974) *Social Work in the Environment*, London, HMSO.

Davies, M. and Knopf, A. (1973) *Social Enquiry Reports and the Probation Service*, London, HMSO.

Davies, M. and Wright, A. (1989) *The Changing Face of Probation: Skills, Knowledge and Qualities in Probation Practice*, Norwich, University of East Anglia.

Davies, H. and Lister, M. (1992) *Evaluation of Offending Behaviour Groups*, Birmingham, West Midlands Probation Service.

Day, N. (1988) 'Area accommodation strategies: a partnership approach to housing for homeless offenders', *Probation Journal*, 35, 110–13.

de la Motta, K. (1984) *Blacks in the Criminal Justice System*, unpublished MSc thesis, University of Aston.

Denman, G. (1982) *Intensive Intermediate Treatment with Juvenile Offenders: A Handbook of Assessment and Groupwork Practice*, Lancaster, Centre of Youth, Crime and Community, Lancaster University.

Denney, D. (1992) *Racism and Anti-Racism in Probation*, London, Routledge.

Department of Health and Social Security (1987) *Reports for Courts: Practice Guidance for Social Workers*, London, HMSO.

Divine, D. (1989) *Towards Real Communication*, Unpublished research report to the West Midlands Probation Service.

Doherty, R., Farrell, D., Flood, E. and Milner, J. M. (1990) 'South Glamorgan's alcohol interventions unit', *Probation Journal*, 37, 23–5.

Dominelli, L. (1984) 'Differential justice: domestic labour, community service and women offenders', *Probation Journal*, 30, 2, 43–9.

Dominelli, L. (1988) *Anti-Racist Social Work*, London, Macmillan.

Drakeford, M. (1983) 'Probation: containment or liberty?', *Probation Journal*, 30, 7–10.

Evans, R. (1991) 'Police cautioning and the young adult offender', *Criminal Law Review* (August), 598–609.

Evans, R. and Wilkinson, C. (1990) 'Variations in police cautioning, policy and practice in England and Wales', *Howard Journal of Criminal Justice*, 29, 155–76.

Fabiano, E., Robinson, D. and Porporino, F. (1990) *A Preliminary Assessment of the Cognitive Skills Training Programme*, Ottawa, Correctional Service of Canada.

Farrington, D. P. (1990) 'Implications of career research for the prevention of offending', *Journal of Adolescence*, 13, 93–113.

Farrington, D. P., Gallagher, B., Morley, L., St Ledger, R. J. and West, D. J. (1986) 'Unemployment, school leaving and crime', *British Journal of Criminology*, 26, 335–56.

Faulkner, D. (1986), speech to a probation service conference, unpublished.

Field, S. (1990) *Trends in Crime and their Interpretation* (Home Office Research Study 119), London, HMSO.

Findlay, J., Bright, J. and Gill, K. (1990) *Youth Crime Prevention: A Handbook of Good Practice*, Swindon, Crime Concern.

Folkard, M. S., Smith, D. E. and Smith, D. D. (1976) *IMPACT Vol II: The Results of the Experiment*, London, HMSO.

Foren, R. and Bailey, R. (1968) *Authority in Social Casework*, Oxford, Pergamon Press.

Forrester, D., Chatterton, M. and Pease, K. (1988) *The Kirkholt Burglary Prevention Project, Rochdale* (Crime Prevention Unit Paper 13), London, Home Office.

Forrester, D., Frenz, S., O'Connell, M. and Pease, K. (1990) *The Kirkholt Burglary Prevention Project Phase II* (Crime Prevention Unit Paper 23), London, Home Office.

French, J. R. P. and Raven, B. (1959) 'The bases of social power', in Cartwright, D. (ed.) *Studies in Social Power*, Ann Arbor, Institute for Social Research.

Frude, N., Honess, T. and Maguire, M. (1990) *CRIME-PICS Handbook*, Cardiff, Michael and Associates.

Fryer, P. (1984) *Staying Power: The History of Black People in Britain*, London, Pluto Press.

Galbraith, J. K. (1992) *The Culture of Contentment*, London, Sinclair-Stevenson.

Gelsthorpe, L. R. (1991) *Race and gender considerations in the preparation and interpretation of social inquiry reports*, report to the Home Office Research and Planning Unit.

Gelsthorpe, L. R. and Raynor, P. (1992) 'The quality of reports prepared in the pilot studies', in J. Bredar (ed.) *Justice Informed*, Vol. II, London, Vera Institute of Justice.

Gelsthorpe, L. R., Raynor, P. and Tisi, A. (1992) *Quality assurance in pre-sentence reports*, report to the Home Office Research and Planning Unit.

Gendreau, P. and Ross, R. R. (1979) 'Effective correctional treatment: bibliotherapy for cynics', *Crime and Delinquency*, 25, 463–89.

Geraghty, J. (1991) *Probation Practice in Crime Prevention* (Crime Prevention Unit Paper 24), London, Home Office.

Haines, K. (1990) *After-Care for Released Prisoners: A Review of the Literature*, Cambridge, Institute of Criminology.

Harris, R. (1989) 'Social work in society or punishment in the community?' in Shaw, R. and Haines, K. (eds) *The Criminal Justice System: A Central Role for the Probation Service*, Cambridge, Institute of Criminology.

Harris, R. (1992) *Crime, Criminal Justice and the Probation Service*, London, Routledge.

Harris, R. and Webb, D. (1987) *Welfare, Power and Juvenile Justice*, London, Tavistock.

Haxby, D. (1978) *Probation: A Changing Service*, London, Constable.

Hayes, M. (1989) 'Promotion and management: what choice for women?', *Probation Journal*, 36, 1, 12–17.

Henderson, P. (1987) *Community Work and the Probation Service*, London, National Institute of Social Work.

Herbert, L and Mathieson, D. (1975) *Reports for Courts*, London, NAPO.

Hine, J., McWilliams, W. and Pease, K. (1978) 'Recommendations, social information and sentencing', *Howard Journal*, 17, 91–100.

Home Office (1961) *Report of the Inter-Departmental Committee on the Business of the Criminal Courts* (the Streatfeild Report) (Cmnd 1289), London, HMSO.

Home Office (1963) *The Organisation of After-Care: Report of the Council on the Treatment of Offenders*, London, HMSO.

Home Office (1974) *Report of the Advisory Council on the Penal System*, London, HMSO.

Home Office (1980) *Young Offenders* (Cmnd 8045), London, HMSO.

Home Office (1984) *Probation Service in England and Wales: Statement of National Objectives and Priorities*, London, Home Office.

Home Office (1986) *Social Inquiry Reports* (Circular 92/1986), London, Home Office.

Home Office (1988) *Punishment, Custody and the Community* (Cm 424), London, HMSO.

Home Office (1990a) *Crime, Justice and Protecting the Public* (Cm 965), London, HMSO.

Home Office (1990b) *Supervision and Punishment in the Community* (Cm 966), London, HMSO.

Home Office (1990c) *Partnership in Dealing with Offenders in the Community*, London, Home Office.

Home Office (1990d) *Partnership in Crime Prevention*, London, Home Office.

Home Office (1990e) *Management Structure Review*, London, Home Office.

Home Office (1991a) *Organising Supervision and Punishment in the Community*, London, Home Office.

Home Office (1991b) *Prison Disturbances April 1990* (Cm 1456) (the Woolf Report), London, HMSO.

Home Office (1992a) *Partnership in Dealing with Offenders in the Community. A Decision Document*, London, Home Office.

Home Office (1992b) *The Probation Service: Statement of Purpose* (draft), London, Home Office.

Home Office (1992c) *National Standards for the Supervision of Offenders in the Community*, London, Home Office.

Home Office (1992d) *The Criminal Justice Act 1991: Training Materials for the Probation Service*, London, Home Office.

Home Office (1992e) *Annual Report 1991* (Cm 1909), London, HMSO.

Hope, T. (1985) *Implementing Crime Prevention Measures* (Home Office Research Study 86), London, HMSO.

Horsley, G. (1984) *The Language of Social Inquiry Reports*, Norwich, University of East Anglia.

Hough, M. and Mayhew, P. (1983) *The British Crime Survey: First Report* (Home Office Research Study 76), London, HMSO.

Hough, M. and Mayhew, P. (1985) *Taking Account of Crime: Key Findings from the 1984 British Crime Survey* (Home Office Research Study 85), London, HMSO.

Hudson, B. (1987) *Justice through Punishment*, London, Macmillan.

Hudson, B. (1988) 'Social skills training in practice', *Probation Journal*, 35, 3, 85–91.

Hugman, B. (1977) *Act Natural: A New Sensibility for the Professional Helper*, London, Bedford Square Press.

Hugman, B. (1980) 'Radical practice in probation' in Brake, M. and Bailey, R. (eds) *Radical Social Work and Practice*, London, Edward Arnold.

Humphrey, C. and Pease, K. (1992) 'Effectiveness measurement in the probation service: a view from the troops', *Howard Journal of Criminal Justice*, 31, 1, 31–52.

Husain S. and Bright, J. (1990) (eds) *Neighbourhood Watch and the Police*, Swindon, Crime Concern.

Jenkins, J. and Lawrence, D. (1992) *Black Groups Initiative Review*, unpublished paper, Inner London Probation Service.

Johnson, D. W. and Johnson, F. P. (1991) *Joining Together: Group Theory and Group Skills*, Englewood Cliffs, N. J., Prentice Hall.

Jones, M., Mordecai, M., Rutter, F. and Thomas, L. (1991) 'A Miskin model of group work with women offenders', *Groupwork*, 4, 215–30.

Jordan, B. (1989) *The Common Good*, Oxford, Blackwell.

Jordan, B. (1990) *Social Work in an Unjust Society*, Hemel Hempstead, Harvester Wheatsheaf.

Jordan, B. and Jones, M. (1988) 'Poverty, the underclass and probation practice', *Probation Journal*, 35, 123–7.

Kent Probation and After-Care Service (1981) 'Probation Control Unit: a community-based experiment in intensive supervision' in *Annual Report on the Work of the Medway Centre*, Maidstone, Kent P.A.C.S.

Kett, J., Collett, S., Barron, C., Hill, I. and Metherell, D. (1992) *Managing and Developing Anti-Racist Practice within Probation: A Resource Pack for Action*, Liverpool, Merseyside Probation Service Resource and Information Unit.

King, J. F. S. (1958) (ed.) *The Probation Service*, London, Butterworth.

King, M. (1988) *How to Make Social Crime Prevention Work: The French Experience*, London, NACRO.

Laycock, G. and Pease, K. (1985) 'Crime prevention within the probation service', *Probation Journal*, 32, 43–7.

Lewis, P. (1991) 'Learning from industry: macho management or collaborative culture', *Probation Journal*, 38, 81–5.

Liebmann, M. (1991) 'Letting go and getting framed', *Probation Journal*, 29, 19–23.

Lipsey, M. W. (1990) 'Juvenile delinquency treatment: a meta-analytic inquiry into the variability of effects'. Paper presented to the 2nd European Conference on Law and Psychology, Universitat Erlangen, Nurnberg.

Lipton, D., Martinson, R. and Wilks, J. (1975) *The Effectiveness of Correctional Treatment*, New York, Praeger.

Lucas, J., Raynor, P. and Vanstone, M. (1992) *Straight Thinking on Probation One Year On: the second report of the evaluation study*, Bridgend, Mid-Glamorgan Probation Service.

MacIntyre, A. (1988) *Whose Justice? Which Rationality?* London, Duckworth.

Mair, G. (1986) 'Ethnic minorities, probation and the magistrates' courts: a pilot study', *British Journal of Criminology*, 26, 147–55.

Mair, G. and Brockington, N. (1988) 'Female offenders and the probation service', *Howard Journal of Criminal Justice*, 27, 117–26.

Marshall, T. F. and Merry, S. (1990) *Crime and Accountability*, London, HMSO.

Martinson, R. (1974) 'What works? Questions and answers about prison reform', *The Public Interest*, 35, 22–54.

Martinson, R. (1979) 'New findings, new views: a note of caution regarding sentencing reform', *Hofstra Law Review*, 7, 243–58.

Mathiesen, T. (1990) *Prison on Trial*, London, Sage.

Mathieson, D. (1979) 'Change in the probation service: implications and effects', in King, J. (ed.) *Pressures and Change in the Probation Service*, Cambridge, Institute of Criminology.

Matza, D. (1964) *Delinquency and Drift*, New York, Wiley.

May, T. (1991) *Probation: Politics, Policy and Practice*, Buckingham, Open University Press.

Mayhew, P., Clarke, R. V. G., Sturman, A. and Hough, J. M. (1976) *Crime as Opportunity* (Home Office Research Study 34), London, HMSO.

Mayhew, P., Elliott, D. and Dowds, L. (1989) *The 1988 British Crime Survey* (Home Office Research Study 111), London, HMSO.

McGuire, J. (1978) *Sheffield Day Training Centre Programme Development: A Report*, Sheffield, South Yorkshire Probation Service.

McGuire, J. (1991) 'Testing Ross's "Reasoning and Rehabilitation" model in Mid-Glamorgan', paper presented at the 'Effectiveness Seminar', Green College, Oxford.

McGuire, J. and Pointing, J. (1988) *Victims of Crime: A New Deal?*, Milton Keynes, Open University Press.

McGuire, J. and Priestley, P. (1990) 'Some things do work', Paper presented to the 2nd European Conference on Law and Psychology, Universitat Erlangen, Nurnberg.

McIvor, G. (1990) *Sanctions for Serious or Persistent Offenders: A Review of the Literature*, Stirling, Social Work Research Centre, University of Stirling.

McIvor, G. (1991) 'Social work intervention in community service', *British Journal of Social Work*, 21, 591–609.

McIvor, G. (1992) *Sentenced to Serve*, Aldershot, Avebury.

McWilliams, W (1980) *Management Models and the Bases of Management Structures*, Unpublished mimeograph.

McWilliams, W. (1983) 'The mission to the English police courts 1876–1936, *Howard Journal of Penology and Crime Prevention* 22, 3, 129–47.

McWilliams, W. (1985) 'The mission transformed: professionalisation of probation between the wars', *Howard Journal of Criminal Justice*, 24, 257–74.

McWilliams, W. (1987) 'Probation, pragmatism and policy', *Howard Journal of Criminal Justice*, 26, 97–121.

McWilliams, W. (1989) 'An expressive model for evaluating probation practice', *Probation Journal*, 36, 58–64.

McWilliams, W. and Pease, K. (1990) 'Probation practice and an end to punishment', *Howard Journal of Criminal Justice*, 29, 14–24.

Monger, M. (1972) *Casework in Probation* (2nd ed.), London, Butterworth.

Morris, A. and Giller, H. (1987) *Understanding Juvenile Justice*, London, Croom Helm.

Mott, J. (1977) 'Decision making and social inquiry reports in one juvenile court', *British Journal of Social Work*, 7, 421–32.

Moxon, D. (1988) *Sentencing in the Crown Court* (Home Office Research Study 103), London, HMSO.

NACRO (1991a) *Replacing Custody*, London, NACRO.

NACRO (1991b) *Youth Crime Prevention: A Coordinated Approach*, London, NACRO.

NACRO (1991c) *Preventing Youth Crime* (Juvenile Crime Committee Policy Paper 30), London, NACRO.

Nation, D. and Arnott, J. (1991) 'House burglars and victims', *Probation Journal* 38, 2, 63–7.

National Audit Office (1989) *Home Office Control and Management of Probation Services in England and Wales*, London, HMSO.

Nelson-Jones, R. (1983) *Basic Counselling Skills*, London, Holt, Rinehart and Winston.

Northumbria Probation Service (1989) *Social Enquiry Report Gatekeeping and Monitoring within the Northumbria Probation Area*, report of an inspection, Newcastle upon Tyne, Northumbria Probation Service.

Paley, J., Thomas, J. and Norman, G. (1986) *Rethinking Youth Social Work*, Leicester, National Youth Bureau.

Pearson, G., Sampson, A., Blagg, H., Stubbs, P. and Smith, D. (1989) 'Policing racism', in Morgan, R. and Smith, D. J. (eds) *Coming to terms with Policing*, London, Routledge, 118–37.

Peelo, M., Stewart, J., Stewart, G. and Prior, A. (1992) *A Sense of Justice: Offenders as Victims of Crime*, Wakefield, ACOP.

Perry, F. (1974) *Information for the Court*, Cambridge, Institute of Criminology.

Petersilia, J. (1990) 'Conditions that permit intensive supervision programmes to survive', *Crime and Delinquency*, 36, 126–45.

Pinder, R. (1982) 'On what grounds? Negotiating justice with black clients', *Probation Journal*, 29, 19–23.

Pratt, J. (1985) 'Delinquency as a scarce resource', *Howard Journal of Criminal Justice*, 24, 81–92.

Priestley, P., McGuire, J., Flegg, D., Hemsley, V. and Welham, D. (1978) *Social Skills and Personal Problem-Solving: A Handbook of Methods*, London, Tavistock.

Priestley, P and McGuire, J. (1985) *Offending Behaviour; Skills and Stratagems for Going Straight*, London, Batsford.

Raven, B. and Kruglanski, A. W. (1970) 'Conflict and power', in Swingle, P. (ed.) *The Structure of Conflict*, New York, Academic Press.

Raynor, P. (1980) 'Is there any sense in social inquiry reports?', *Probation Journal*, 27, 78–84.

Raynor, P. (1984) 'Evaluation with one eye closed: the empiricist agenda in social work research', *British Journal of Social Work*, 14, 1–10.

Raynor, P. (1985) *Social Work, Justice and Control*, Oxford, Blackwell.

Raynor, P. (1988) *Probation as an Alternative to Custody*, Aldershot, Avebury.

Raynor, P. (1990) 'Measuring effectiveness in a principled probation service', in *Assessing the Effectiveness of Probation Practice: Proceedings of the 1988 Probation Research and Information Exchange*, Sheffield, University of Sheffield.

Raynor, P. (1991) 'Sentencing with and without reports: a local study', *Howard Journal of Criminal Justice*, 30, 293–300.

Raynor, P. and Vanstone, M. (1992a) 'STOP Start', *Social Work Today*, 16 February, 26–7.

Raynor, P. and Vanstone, M. (1992b) *Straight Thinking on Probation: first interim report of the evaluation study*, Swansea, Mid-Glamorgan Probation Service and Centre for Applied Social Studies.

Reeves, H. (1984) 'The victim and reparation', *Probation Journal* 31, 136–9.

Riley, D. and Tuck, M. (1986) 'The theory of reasoned action', in Cornish, D. B. and Clarke, R. V. G. (eds) *The Reasoning Criminal*, Berlin, Springer-Verlag.

Roberts, C. H. (1989) *First Evaluation Report, Young Offenders Project*, Worcester, Hereford and Worcester Probation Service.

Rock, P. (1990) *Help for Victims of Crime*, Oxford, Clarendon Press.

Rosenbaum, D. P. (1988) 'A critical eye on neighbourhood watch: does it reduce crime and fear?' in Hope, T. and Shaw, M. (eds) *Communities and Crime Reduction*, London, HMSO.

Ross, R. R. and Fabiano, E. A. (1985) *Time to Think: A Cognitive Model of Delinquency Prevention and Offender Rehabilitation*, Johnson City, Academy of Arts and Sciences.

Ross, R. R., Fabiano, E. A. and Ewles, C. D. (1988) 'Reasoning and Rehabilitation', *International Journal of Offender Therapy and Comparative Criminology*, 32, 29–35.

Ross, R. R., Fabiano, E. A. and Ross, R. (1989) *Reasoning and Rehabilitation: a handbook for teaching cognitive skills*, Ottawa, The Cognitive Centre.

Rumgay, J. (1989) 'Talking tough: empty threats in probation practice', *Howard Journal of Criminal Justice*, 28, 177–86.

Rutherford, A. (1986) *Growing Out of Crime*, Harmondsworth, Penguin.

Sampson, A. (1991) *Lessons from a Victim Support Crime Prevention Project* (Crime Prevention Unit Paper 25), London, Home Office.

Sampson, A., Stubbs, P., Smith, D., Pearson, G. and Blagg, H. (1988) 'Crime, localities and the multi-agency approach', *British Journal of Criminology*, 28, 473–93.

Sampson, A., Smith., D., Pearson, G., Blagg, H. and Stubbs, P. (1991) 'Gender issues in inter-agency relations: police, probation and social services', in Abbott, P. and Wallace, C. (eds) *Gender, Sexuality and Power*, London, Macmillan, 114–32.

Sampson, A. and Smith, D. (1992) 'Probation and community crime prevention', *Howard Journal of Criminal Justice*, 31, 105–19.

Scott, D., Stone, N., Simpson, P. and Falkingham, P. (1985) (eds) *Going Local in Probation?*, Norwich and Manchester, Social Work Programme, University of East Anglia and Department of Social Administration, University of Manchester.

Sheldon, B. (1984) 'Evaluation with one eye closed: the empiricist agenda in social work research – a reply to Peter Raynor', *British Journal of Social Work*, 14, 635–7.

Singer, L. R. (1991) 'A non-punitive paradigm for probation practice: some sobering thoughts', *British Journal of Social Work*, 21, 611–26.

Smith, D. (1987) 'The limits of positivism in social work research', *British Journal of Social Work*, 17, 401–16.

Smith, D. (1992) 'Making a success of inter-agency work', *The Magistrate*, June, 94.

Smith, D., Blagg, H. and Derricourt, N. (1988) 'Mediation in South Yorkshire', *British Journal of Criminology*, 28, 378–95.

Smith, D., Paylor, I. and Mitchell, P. (1993) 'Partnerships between the independent sector and the probation service', *Howard Journal of Criminal Justice*, 32, 25–39.

Smith, J. P. (1990) *Change and New Directions in the Probation Service: The Development of the Practice and Concept of Mediation*, unpublished PhD thesis, Sheffield City Polytechnic.

Smith, S. J. (1986) *Crime, Space and Society*, Cambridge, Cambridge University Press.

Stewart, G., Stewart, J., Prior, A. and Peelo, M. (1989) *Surviving Poverty: Probation Work and Benefits Policy*, Wakefield, ACOP.

Tarling, R. (1979) *Sentencing Practice in Magistrates' Courts* (Home Office Research Study 56), London, HMSO.

Thomas, R. and Vanstone, M. (1992) 'Leadership in the middle', *Probation Journal*, 39, 19–23.

Thornton, D., Curran, L., Grayson, D. and Holloway, V. (1984) *Tougher Regimes in Detention Centres*, London, HMSO.

Thorpe, D. H., Smith, D., Green, C. J. and Paley, J. H. (1980) *Out of Care: The Community Support of Juvenile Offenders*, London, Allen and Unwin.

Thorpe, J. (1979) *Social Inquiry Reports: A Survey* (Home Office Research Study 48), London, HMSO.

Tuck, M. (1987) 'Crime prevention: a shift in concept', *Home Office Research and Planning Unit Research Bulletin No. 25*, London, Home Office.

Tutt, N. and Giller, H. (1984) *Social Inquiry Reports*, Lancaster, Social Information Systems (audiotape).

Vanstone, M. (1986) 'The Pontypridd Day Training Centre: diversion from prison in action', in Pointing, J. (ed.) *Alternatives to Custody*, Oxford, Blackwell.

Vanstone, M. (1987) 'Keeping in professional shape: a collaborative strategy for skill development', *Probation Journal*, 34, 132–4.

Vanstone, M. (1988) 'Values, leadership and the future of the probation service', *Probation Journal*, 35, 131–4.

Vanstone, M. (1993) 'A "missed opportunity" reassessed: the influence of the Day Training Centre experiment on the criminal justice system and probation practice', *British Journal of Social Work*, 23, 3, 213–29.

Vanstone, M. and Raynor, P. (1981) 'Diversion from prison – a partial success and a missed opportunity', *Probation Journal*, 28, 85–9.

Vanstone, M. and Seymour, B. (1986) 'Probation service objectives and the neglected ingredients', *Probation Journal*, 33, 43–8.

Vass, A. A. (1990) *Alternatives to Prison*, London, Sage.

Vass, A. and Weston, A. (1990) 'Probation day centres as alternatives to custody; a "Trojan horse" examined', *British Journal of Criminology*, 30, 189–206.

Walker, H. and Beaumont, B. (1981) *Probation Work: Critical Theory and Socialist Practice*, Oxford, Blackwell.

Walker, H. and Beaumont, B. (1985) (eds) *Working with Offenders*, London, Macmillan.

Walker, N. Farrington, D. P. and Tucker, G. (1981) 'Reconviction rates of adult males after different sentences', *British Journal of Criminology*, 21, 4, 357–60.

Weaver, C. and Fox, C. (1984) 'Berkeley sex offenders group: a seven year evaluation', *Probation Journal*, 31, 143–6.

Weston, W. R. (1973) 'Style of management in the probation and after-care service', *Probation Journal*, 20, 69–73.

Whitehouse, P. (1983) 'Race, bias and social enquiry reports, *Probation Journal*, 30, 2, 43–9.

Williams, B. (1992) *Work with Prisoners*, Birmingham, Venture Press.

Willis, A. (1986) 'Alternatives to imprisonment: an elusive paradise', in Pointing, J. (ed.) *Alternatives to Custody*, Oxford, Blackwell.

Willis, C. (1983) *The Use, Effectiveness and Impact of Police Stop and Search Powers* (Home Office Research and Planning Unit paper 15), London, Home Office.

Winnicott, C. (1962) 'Casework and agency function', *Case Conference*, 8, 174–84.

Worrall, A. (1990) *Offending Women: Female Lawbreakers and the Criminal Justice System*, London, Routledge.

Young, J. (1991) 'Ten points of realism', in Young, J. and Matthews, R. (eds) *Rethinking Criminology: The Realist Debate*, London, Sage.

Index

172